Published in Nashville, Tennessee, by Thomas Nelson. Thomas Nelson is a trademark of Thomas Nelson, Inc.

Thomas Nelson, Inc. titles may be purchased in bulk for educational, business, fund-raising, or sales promotional use. For information, please e-mail SpecialMarkets@ThomasNelson.com.

Printed in the United States of America

07 08 09 10 11 12 13 14 15—9 8 7 6 5 4 3 2 1

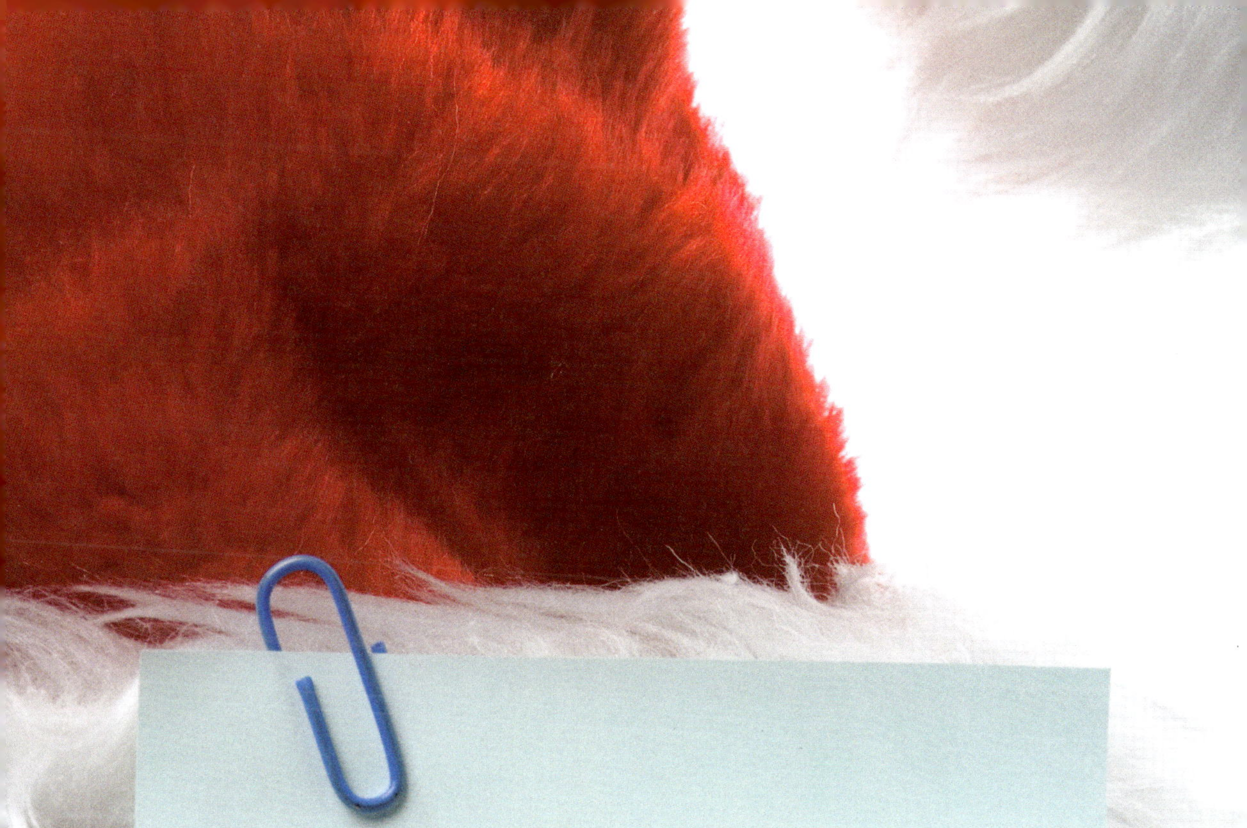

Dear Lover of Christmas,

Welcome to **Christmas A to Z**—your key to unwrapping the wonder of hundreds of seasonal words and phrases. Within these pages, you'll enter the world of everything Christmas to discover the traditions and the trivia surrounding this holy and happy holiday season.

We trust that you'll delight in sharing your journey into Christmas with everyone you know!

Merry Christmas to you and yours,
The Publisher

A Christmas Carol

Charles Dickens first published *A Christmas Carol in Prose, Being a Ghost Story of Christmas* in 1843, but it has come to be known simply as *A Christmas Carol*. The author himself referred to it as "the little carol" and compared it to a song celebrating the Christmas season; he even referred to the chapters as "staves" (a musical term). To quote Dickens, "I have endeavored in this ghostly little book to raise the ghost of an idea which shall not put my readers out of humor with themselves, with each other, with the season or with me." *A Christmas Carol* is a Victorian morality play about a penny-pinching miser named Ebenezer Scrooge who finds redemption after he is confronted with a trio of ghosts (Christmas Past, Present, and Future) on Christmas Eve. Charles Dickens was concerned about the education and care of the poor people of England (he had been one of them). He had written pamphlets and given talks on the subject; but through *A Christmas Carol*, he reached a worldwide audience and will continue to reach them for generations to come. *A Christmas Carol* has been adapted to film, television, and radio, with perhaps the most critically acclaimed film version being the 1951 British version entitled *Scrooge* and starring Alistair Sim. It has become one of the most enduring Christmas stories of all time.

A Christmas Story

A Christmas Story is a film, which has gained considerable popularity since its debut in 1983. Based on the semi-autobiographical writings of writer/actor Jean Shepherd (who also narrated the film), the central character is Ralphie Parker, a boy who wants more than anything for Santa to bring him a Red Ryder BB gun for Christmas, in spite of his parents' warnings that he will shoot his eye out. *A Christmas Story* was a sleeper hit, which received very little fanfare when it debuted but which has found its own place in the hearts of people who love the film (some television stations air 24-hour back-to-back showings of the movie at Christmastime). The home featured in the movie has been lovingly restored exactly as it appeared in the film and is now a major tourist attraction in Cleveland, Ohio. And a replica of Old Man Parker's "major award" is now available for purchase for truly die-hard fans of the film (*see* Leg Lamp).

Abide

To abide is to remain, to stay, to continue (*abide with me*). It can also mean to wait for something (*to abide the coming of the Lord*). In legal terms, to abide by something means to be obedient to or act in accordance with (*to abide by the court's ruling*).

Abominable Snowman

Also known as the Yeti, the Abominable Snowman is the Bigfoot of the Himalayas. The most famous Abominable Snowman is arguably the cartoon character Bumble, the Snow Monster of the North (*see* Rudolph the Red-Nosed Reindeer).

Adore

To adore is to worship, to give divine honor. What a perfect word for the Christmas carol "O Come All Ye Faithful" where the author of the carol urges us, "O come, let us adore Him." The familiar Christmas carol, which is attributed to Englishman John Wade, was originally penned in Latin in the 1740s and called "Adeste Fideles." It wasn't translated to the familiar English version until a century later by Rev. Frederick Oakeley and William Thomas Brooke. The popular carol is rumored to have been the favorite Christmas song of U.S. President Dwight D. Eisenhower.

Advent

The word "advent" stems from *Adventus*, the Latin word for "coming," and refers to the coming of the Savior. In the Christian church, Advent represents the four weeks before Christmas and is considered a holy season. Some families observe Advent with the lighting of candles, one for each of the four Sundays of Advent. Each candle symbolizes a different aspect of the Advent story or theme of the season. The first candle, which is lit on the first Sunday of Advent, represents hope or prophecy; the final candle, called the Christ Candle, is often lit on Christmas Eve or Christmas Day.

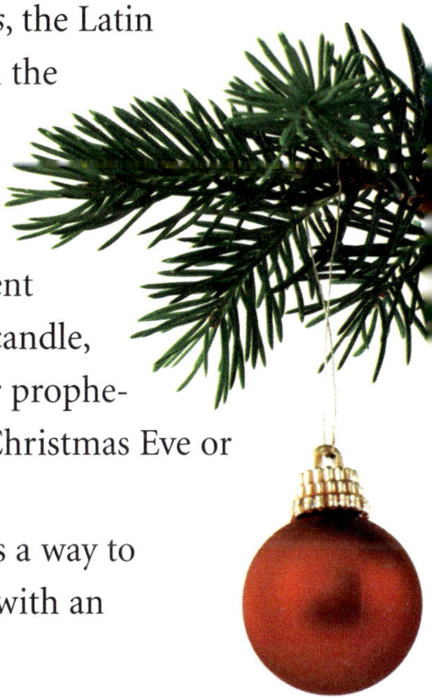

Many children look forward to the Advent calendar as a way to mark the season. Another popular way to observe Advent is with an Advent wreath.

Trivia

What would happen if you ate a poinsettia plant?

a. You'd get stained teeth and a not-so-delicious meal.
b. You'd die.
c. You'd grow a red nose like Rudolph.
d. You'd have stomach problems for a couple of days.

Advent Wreath

The Advent wreath can be a home-based family craft consisting of the candles of Advent, together with evergreens to make a wreath which symbolizes eternity. The Advent wreath consists of four candles—traditionally, three of the candles have been violet and one rose-colored, but it is now acceptable to use four violet candles. Some churches use blue candles and reserve the violet candles for Lent. The first candle, which is lit on the first Sunday of Advent, represents the hope of Jesus' arrival and is sometimes called the prophet's candle. The second candle, which is lit on the second Sunday of Advent, is generally called the Bethlehem candle. The third Sunday of Advent is observed with the shepherd's candle, and the fourth Sunday of Advent is observed by the lighting of the angel's candle. Some use a center candle, generally white, which is lit on Christmas Eve or Christmas Day and which symbolizes Christ's birth.

Answer: D. Contrary to popular belief, the poinsettia is not deadly, but you would regret having eaten one.

Alleluia

"Alleluia" is the Greek form of the word "Hallelujah," which is sometimes translated as "Praise the Lord." Since it appears most often in Scripture in the Book of Psalms, it may originally have been a call to worship. For many Christians, "Hallelujah" is a joyful expression of praise to God.

Aluminum

Aluminum Christmas trees were introduced in the late 1950s. It was the dawn of the Space Age, and families were drawn to the novelty and convenience of the artificial tree, yet the green artificial trees of the period were not very realistic or aesthetically pleasing. It was the decade of the Hula Hoop, and consumers were ready for something exciting and new. Thus the aluminum Christmas tree was born—a Space Age tree if ever there was one.

During the 10 years or so that the trees were in vogue, they were manufactured in a variety of sizes and colors, from the popular shiny silver to gold, red, pink, green, and blue. Shoppers could also purchase a rotating color wheel, which projected a different color onto the tree every few seconds. You could even purchase a rotating Christmas tree stand. There has been a resurgence of popularity of the retro aluminum tree during the past few years, and if you find one complete with its color wheel, a collector of 1950s nostalgia would tell you that you've found a treasure. No matter how much you may love your traditional tree, a rotating aluminum tree, complete with the magic of a color wheel, will bring a smile to the Baby Boomer who recalls Christmas past.

Angel

An angel is a supernatural spiritual being who, according to Scripture, is superior to human beings in strength and intelligence (one angel can slay 10,000 men). Yet Scripture also tells us that the angels long to peer into the things concerning us. They have freedom of choice—some have chosen to follow God, and fallen angels (those who sinned against God) have chosen to follow Satan. Angels frequently appear as messengers of God and are guardians of human beings. They often appear at important events in human history, most notably to the shepherds on the night the Savior was born. Some people are very wary about turning away the stranger, for who knows but that in doing so an angel may be turned away?

Angel Tree

An angel tree is a Christmas tree that contains cards describing the wishes of individuals who need assistance during the holidays. While many churches and organizations sponsor angel trees, you can find one almost anywhere during the Christmas season, including your local grocery store or shopping mall. Donors choose a card from the tree and make a commitment to purchase needed items (such as clothing or toys) for the individual or family whose card they have taken. An angel tree is a wonderful way for parents to teach their children that Christmas is about giving, not just receiving.

Anna

According to Scripture, the prophetess Anna was often to be found at the temple serving God with prayers and fasting. She was an elderly widow, and she longed to see the Messiah with her own eyes before she died. Her longed-for hope was realized when Joseph and Mary brought the infant Jesus to the temple to be dedicated. Because of Anna's longstanding relationship with God, she recognized the Messiah, even though He was a baby (Luke 2:36–38).

Anthem

An anthem is a form of church music, which can be more elaborate than a hymn and which contains lyrics from Scripture. Early anthems tended to be simple so that the words could be heard clearly. Anthems were originally associated with the Church of England and were introduced in America in the 18th century. The term "anthem" has come to mean a song of celebration (*e.g.*, our National Anthem).

Antiphonal Music

Antiphonal music splits the chorus or instrumentation into left and right halves of equal strength (think of a stereo recording as opposed to monaural). Antiphonal singing, which was developed in monasteries and introduced to the church by St. Ambrose (A.D. 340–397), refers to a singing style in which choruses are alternated (the first chorus sings a phrase and the second chorus sings an answering phrase).

Apostles' Creed

There are many theories about the origin of the Apostles' Creed. There is no doubt, however, that it is centuries old. Whether it was actually written by the apostles themselves is unknown. Some scholars place its creation as early as the first or second century; some place it as late as the ninth century. It may have been formulated to refute Gnosticism. Whatever its origin, it is the most popular creed used in worship by Western Christians. There are slightly different versions of the Apostles' Creed; but in essence, it affirms:

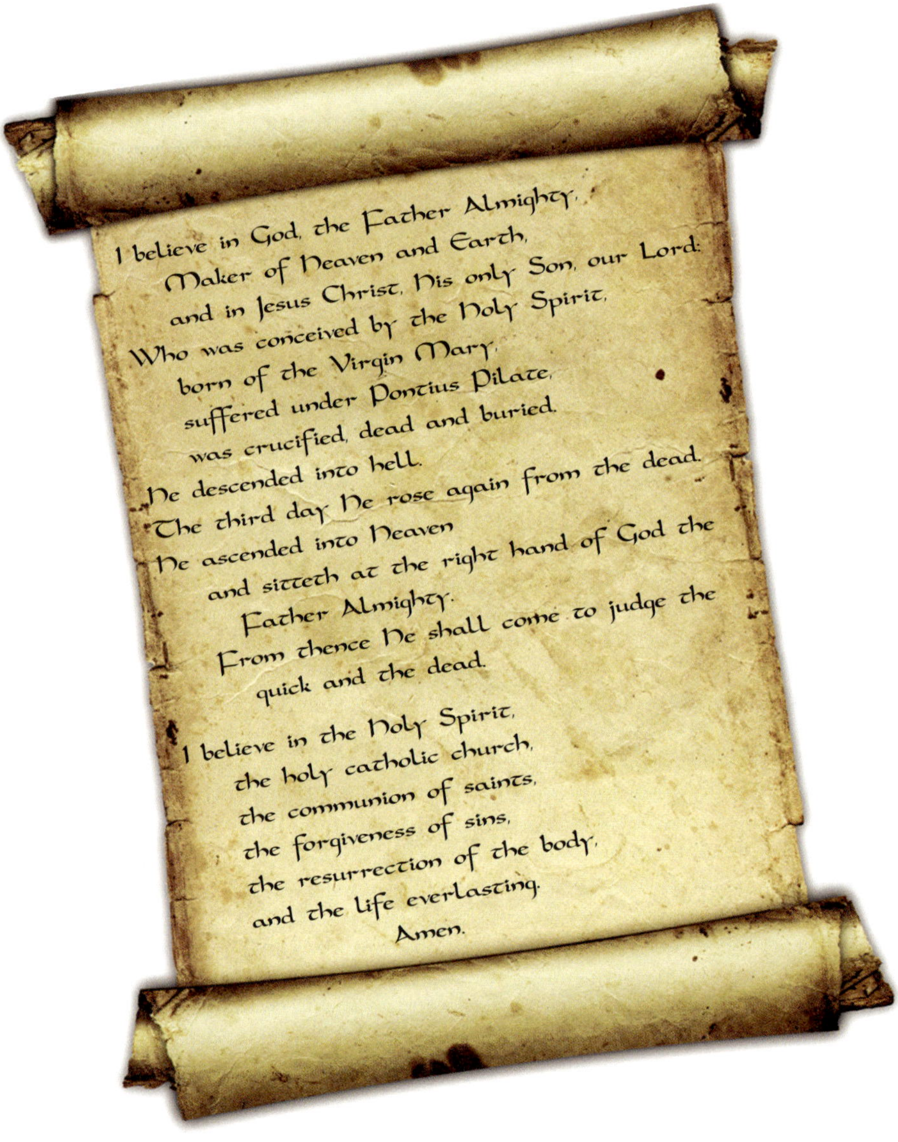

Apparel

In the Christmas carol "Deck the Halls," the listener is encouraged to "Don we now our gay apparel." The music to "Deck the Halls" is believed to be Welsh in origin, dating as far back as the 16th century. Mozart used the tune in the 18th century; however, although the author of the lyrics is unknown, the lyrics are said to have originated in America. Since "apparel" is another word for clothing, the lyricist is encouraging the listener to dress in festive clothing to celebrate the Christmas season.

Apples in Stockings

In simpler times, children would hang their stockings by the fireplace and wake on Christmas morning to find apples, oranges, and nuts in their stockings as a reward from Santa Claus for being a good little boy or girl.

Aramaic Language

Aramaic is most probably the language that was spoken by Jesus (some of the phrases He uttered in Scripture that have been preserved for us were in Aramaic). Aramaic is a group of Semitic languages, still spoken today in some communities (such as Assyrian communities) but considered to be an endangered language. Aramaic is the primary language of the Talmud, and large sections of the biblical books of Daniel and Ezra were written in Aramaic.

Archelaus

Archelaus was the son of Herod the Great and the brother of Herod Antipas. Like his father, Archelaus was cruel; he was responsible for the slaughter of 3,000 people. He inherited the kingdom of Judea from his father but waited to assume the throne until he had petitioned the Roman emperor Augustus. He was opposed in Rome by his brother Antipas, but Augustus gave him the greater part of the kingdom, along with the title ethnarch (governor). He was eventually deposed and banished, and the land over which he had reigned (Judea, Samaria, and Idumea) became the Roman province of Iudaea.

Atonement

Atonement is the reconciliation of God and humankind through the death of His Son, Jesus Christ. Our atonement is the reason Jesus was born into our world. Through His sacrificial death, He has taken our place and paid for our sins, making it possible for us to be forgiven and reinstated as God's children. To "atone" means to become "at one" with. Because of Jesus, we have "at-one-ment" with our God, once we choose to put our faith in His Son and follow Him.

Augustus, Caesar

Gaius Julius Caesar Octavianus (born Gaius Octavius; later known as Octavianus; English, Octavian) was an ambitious Roman who made the best possible use of his tenuous connection to Julius Caesar. When Caesar was killed, Octavius became his heir and used his position as

Caesar's heir to climb to power. While Augustus (a title of honor bestowed upon Octavian) is credited with ending a century of civil wars and ushering in peace for Rome, for which he is regarded as one of the most influential figures in ancient history, this was not a figure who exhibited superiority as much as ambition. This was a man who knew how to make the best of his situation, quash his enemies, and climb to power. He was not cut in the mold of his great-uncle, Julius Caesar. While Julius Caesar had demonstrated clemency in his victories, his adopted son and heir, Octavian, savagely butchered Caesar's son by Queen Cleopatra, Caesarion. He is credited with saying, "Two Caesars are one too many." Mark Antony and Cleopatra took their own lives, rather than fall into captivity to Octavian. Octavian made certain by the slaughter of Julius Caesar's son that he would remain Caesar's only heir. After Octavian's death, the title "Augustus" was given to all Roman emperors (*see* Caesar).

Auld Lang Syne

Most people know the tune to "Auld Lang Syne" and may attempt to follow tradition and sing it on New Year's Eve at midnight, but few know the lyrics. "Auld Lang Syne" is a poem by Robert Burns. Its words may have been inspired by even older folk songs that used the same phrase. Robert Burns claimed to have discovered the song being sung by an old man; but at the time, it was customary to claim certain works to be "traditional" in order to give them a certain cachet. It is doubtful that the melody used today is the same as the poet intended, but there is little doubt that the melody is pure and traditional. It is most likely a Scottish or Northumbrian folk melody; but no matter its origin, the song can be heard worldwide every New Year's Eve.

Trivia

Just what is a sugarplum, exactly?

a. A poetic name for "prune."
b. Caramelized plums, a dessert in the 1800s.
c. A confection made of flavored sugar and fruit or nuts.
d. A brand of lollipops that no longer exists.

Answer: C. A sugarplum is a disk-shaped candy made with fondant.

Babes in Toyland

Babes in Toyland is a 1934 black-and-white film starring Stan Laurel and Oliver Hardy and is based on Victor Herbert's popular 1903 operetta. Actors in this Hal Roach comedy incurred several injuries during the filming, including actor Kewpie Morgan, who played Old King Cole. His part called for him to laugh continuously, causing him to rupture muscles in his stomach. The film has been reissued under various titles, including *March of the Wooden Soldiers*. In 1961, it was remade by Disney and starred Annette Funicello (an original Mouseketeer), Tommy Sands (a pop singer best remembered for marrying Frank Sinatra's daughter Nancy), Ray Bolger (the Scarecrow from the 1939 film *The Wizard of Oz*), and Ed Wynn.

Bah! Humbug!

A humbug is something intended to deceive, a hoax, or a fraud. In more modern times, it has come to mean something that is rubbish or nonsense. The phrase "Bah! Humbug!" was immortalized by Charles Dickens's character Ebenezer Scrooge in *A Christmas Carol* and is jokingly used to express disgust with Christmas or Christmas traditions (*see* A Christmas Carol).

Balthazar / Balthasar

"Balthazar" is a traditional name given to one of the unnamed wise men mentioned in the New Testament. Along with the other wise men, traditionally known as Caspar and Melchior, he followed a star in search of the infant Jesus. Although the New Testament does not specify the number of wise men who traveled together, readers assume there were three because the text mentions three gifts they brought with them. The name "Balthazar" is also a variation on the name "Belshazzar," a Babylonian king who can be found in the Book of Daniel (*see* Magi).

Batteries

The technical definition for a battery is a long-lived dry cell with an alkaline electrolyte that decreases corrosion of the cell. A Mom and Dad definition for a battery is something that prevents disappointed little faces on Christmas morning. So many toys run on batteries that Santa's helpers would do well to remember to add them to the Christmas shopping list and pick them up when making purchases. Most toys will list on their boxes the type of batteries they require, and almost all of them will have the words "batteries not included" somewhere on the packaging. So don't forget to stock up!

Beatitudes, The

"Beatitude" comes from the Latin word for happiness. The Beatitudes are the blessings Jesus pronounced in the opening of the "Sermon on the Mount" in Matthew 5:3–12. Each blessing begins with the phrase "Blessed are. . . ." Some scholars translate each beatitude as an exclamation, such as: "O the bliss of . . . ," which is basically like saying, "Happy are those who . . . ." But Jesus wasn't talking about external, superficial happiness. He was talking about having the deep joy of the soul.

The Beatitudes describe the qualities exhibited in the lives of true disciples. In them, Jesus outlined disciples' rewards, both in this present life and in the life to come. He explained that a true disciple has a character and lifestyle distinct from the world's norm and would not even be considered "blessed" by worldly standards. But in God's economy, a true disciple is blessed and will receive a reward for living a life that pleases Him.

Begotten

To "beget" something is to procreate, sire, or cause to exist. In the New Testament, Jesus is described as God's only begotten Son. In other words, He is unique, singular, one of a kind (John 1:14, 18; 3:16–18; 1 John 4:9).

Belfry

A belfry is a bell tower, either attached to a church or standing on its own; it's the part of a steeple in which the bell is hung. In slang usage, it can refer to the head or mind (such as referring to someone whose ideas seem to be nonsense as "having bats in the belfry").

Believe

If you have confidence or faith in something or someone, if you have an assurance in your heart regarding something or someone, then you believe in that person or thing. The word "believe" is seen more and more frequently in department stores, shopping malls, and trendy little boutiques as an adornment on pillows, Christmas stockings, and other holiday items. The intent is to encourage the beholder to believe in Santa Claus, a fictional being. However, for the Christian, when "believe" adorns a Christmas stocking, pillow, or other seasonal item, the meaning is entirely different. Christians believe in the One whose birthday is celebrated on Christmas Day.

Bells

Bells have long been associated with important occasions, from funerals to weddings. They have become such an integral part of the Christmas season that it's difficult to imagine Christmas without them. In addition to the bell ringers who are often seen on street corners (*see* Salvation Army Bell Ringers), bells have found their way into many of our favorite Christmas carols, from "Jingle Bells" to "Silver Bells." They jingle on our doors, they find their way into our jewelry box in the form of jingle bell earrings or necklaces, and they adorn our packages. Nothing sounds more like Christmas than the ringing of sleigh bells. Bells provide a happy way to usher in the Christmas season and announce the birth of Jesus Christ.

Belly

In a famous Christmas poem, Santa is said to have a "round little belly that shakes when he laughs like a bowl full of jelly." No one can imagine a skinny Santa. He's not working out at the local gym; he's not on the latest diet craze. He's not worried about cholesterol, either the good or the bad kind. In a society that seems to chant the mantra "thin is in," the one notable exception is Santa. No one wants him to diet. No one wants him to be the next successful extreme makeover. We want him to fill out that red suit, and we want him to have a belly. He just wouldn't be Santa without it (*see* Bowl Full of Jelly).

Bethlehem

The city of Bethlehem is located in Israel and is first mentioned in the account of the death of Rachel (Genesis 35:19). The tiny town continued to play an important part in the lives of the ancestors of Jesus Christ. Ruth and Boaz met there. The future King David was anointed there. Later referred to as the City of David, Bethlehem had been his ancestral home. Most importantly, Jesus was born there, fulfilling the prophecy that proclaimed His birth in Bethlehem (Micah 5:2). Jesus, the Bread of Life, was born in Bethlehem, which means "House of Bread."

Betrothal

In biblical times, a betrothal was a promise or contract for a future marriage (it could be compared to what we term an engagement, but it was much more closely linked with marriage). The most important betrothal mentioned in the Bible was the betrothal of Joseph and Mary, the mother of Jesus. Mary was already betrothed to Joseph when she conceived Jesus by the power of the Holy Spirit. By law, when Mary was found to be with child, Joseph could have ended the engagement and had Mary put to death. Instead, Joseph believed Mary. He chose to marry her; and in so doing, he fulfilled his destiny as the stepfather of Jesus. He loved and cared for Mary and Jesus, and he raised Jesus in a godly home. The importance of Joseph's role in the life of Jesus should not be overlooked.

Betrothed

Engaged to be married (*Mary was betrothed to Joseph*). The person to whom someone is engaged (*Joseph was the betrothed of Mary*).

Bible, The

The Bible is a collection of sacred books uniquely inspired by God. These books contain many stories about God's interaction with humankind, as well as the instructions for how to serve God and love others. In addition to being an unsurpassed collection of wisdom on every topic of life from family to money, the Bible contains all the guidelines for living a truly meaningful life, a life with purpose that will leave a lasting impact.

The Bible is also incredibly unique in the fact that each of its separate books, which were written by more than 30 different people over a period of more than 1,500 years, points to a central theme, a single story unlike any other story ever told. The Bible chronicles the story of a loving God on a continuing quest to win back His creation after all of humankind rebelled against Him to go their own way.

This story culminates with God sending His own Son into the world, to be born in human form in order to become a living example for those who want to be reconciled to God. But God's Son, Jesus, doesn't just point the way back to God; He provides it. He allows His earthly life to be taken. He dies in our place, making complete atonement for all of the sins we commit against God and one another. The Christmas celebration is actually our way of commemorating the day God sent His own Son to be born into the world to provide the way for all to be sons and daughters of God.

Trivia

All these reportedly happened on a December 25, except:

a. St. Francis of Assisi made the first Nativity scene.
b. Ricky Martin was born in San Juan, Puerto Rico.
c. Chuck Woolery left *Wheel of Fortune* after his six-year stint as host.
d. Charles Dickens's *A Christmas Carol* was read on the radio for the first time.

Bible, Books of the

The Bible is made up of two major sections known as the Old Testament and the New Testament. The Old Testament tells the story of human history from the time of Creation until about 400 years before the birth of God's Son, Jesus. The New Testament tells the story of Jesus and the establishment of the early church. Everything in the Old Testament paves the way for the revelation of God's Son in the New Testament.

Answer: B. Ricky Martin's birthday is December 24.

For instance, much of Jesus' life was revealed beforehand to Old Testament prophets. They described the Son of God and the things He would do in great detail hundreds of years before Jesus was born. Even though the spiritual life described in the Old Testament seems very different from the spiritual life described in the New Testament (at least on the surface), the Old and New Testaments are actually parts of exactly the same story. This becomes incredibly clear once we realize that everything in the Bible points to Jesus.

Even though the Bible is bound as a single volume, it is not a single book. It is actually a library of smaller books, which were written over many generations. In fact, the word "Bible" is derived from the Latin term *biblia* meaning "library." The Bible contains books of history, law, prophecy, poetry, Gospels, and even letters written by a few of the Fathers of the early Christian church. Here is a brief look at the types of books in the Bible:

OLD TESTAMENT

The Books of the Law

Genesis
Exodus
Leviticus
Numbers
Deuteronomy

The History of Israel

Joshua
Judges
Ruth
1 Samuel
2 Samuel
1 Kings
2 Kings
1 Chronicles
2 Chronicles
Ezra
Nehemiah
Esther

Poetry or "Wisdom Books"

Job
Psalms
Proverbs
Ecclesiastes
Song of Solomon

Books of Prophecy

Isaiah
Jeremiah
Lamentations
Ezekiel
Daniel
Hosea
Joel
Amos
Obadiah
Jonah
Nahum
Habakkuk
Zephaniah
Haggai
Zechariah
Malachi

NEW TESTAMENT

The Story of Jesus and His Disciples

Matthew
Mark
Luke
John
Acts

Paul's Letters to the Churches

Romans
1 Corinthians
2 Corinthians
Galatians
Ephesians
Philippians
Colossians
1 Thessalonians
2 Thessalonians
1 Timothy
2 Timothy
Titus
Philemon

Other Letters to the Churches

Hebrews	1 John
James	2 John
1 Peter	3 John
2 Peter	Jude

Prophecy

Revelation

Bicycle

If you've ever assembled a bicycle for your child on Christmas Eve (or simply had to sneak one into the house and under the tree), then you belong to that group of unsung heroes and heroines who are brave enough to tackle instructions, tighten gaskets, screw things together, and take things apart, all so a special boy or girl can squeal with delight on Christmas morning. Nothing can compare with receiving your first bike, especially if it's waiting for you under the Christmas tree! So whether it's a shiny red tricycle for a precocious three-year-old, a pink bike with ribbons and training wheels for a princess, or a 10-speed for that adventurous older child, a bicycle can create a very special and enduring Christmas memory.

Bing Crosby

See Crosby, Bing.

Black Friday

Every store and shopping mall in America both looks forward to and dreads Black Friday, the day after Thanksgiving, which traditionally marks the start of the Christmas shopping season. Shoppers invade the malls in droves, lured in by great deals and unconventional hours (many stores open at dawn). While most folks believe this is the busiest shopping day of the season, statistics favor the Saturday just before Christmas. Nevertheless, the savvy consumer will wear her most comfortable shoes, have credit cards ready, and make sure she's covered by insurance, just in case she's trampled by others trying to beat her to the door-busting sales.

Blitzen

Blitzen is the name given to one of Santa's eight reindeer in the classic 1800s poem, *A Visit from St. Nicholas* (more commonly known as *'Twas the Night Before Christmas*). Traditionally, the poem has been attributed to Clement C. Moore but some experts believe that it was actually written by Henry Livingston, Jr. Blitzen was originally "Blixem" (Dutch) but was changed by Moore in later versions to the German Blitzen, which means lightning. Blitzen makes a more contemporary appearance in the popular Christmas song from 1949 "Rudolph the Red-Nosed Reindeer," sung by Gene Autry (*see* Rudolph the Red-Nosed Reindeer).

Blood

There are a number of Christmas symbols that represent different aspects of the life and death of Jesus Christ, such as the red stripes in the candy cane, which represent His blood that was shed for us, as do holly's red berries. The traditional colors of Christmas are red and green. The richness of the color red reminds us at Christmas of the sacrifice that Jesus made for us and of God's eternal love for us in sending His precious Son.

Blue

The color blue is used throughout the Old Testament. It is one of the colors described as being part of the holy covering or hangings in the holy places. It is also a color used to distinguish wealth, although not used as frequently as purple (Exodus 26:1, 36; 27:16; 28:8, 31).

Blue Christmas

While Elvis Presley was not the first artist to record "Blue Christmas," his version of the song has become a holiday staple. When Elvis recorded it in 1957 for his LP *Elvis' Christmas Album,* he omitted a verse that had been included by country artist Ernest Tubb in his 1948 version of the song. Driving by a house decorated at Christmastime all in blue lights, it's easy to remember Elvis's heartbroken refrain.

Boar's Head

The boar's head tradition is an ancient British custom in which a boar was sacrificed for the Yuletide feast. Its head was carried into the medieval banquet hall, resplendent on a silver or gold platter and sporting an apple in its mouth. During the procession, minstrels played tunes and a boar's head carol was sung. Think of it as a medieval version of serving the Christmas ham or turkey.

Boiled Custard

Egg and milk custards are of ancient origin (a Roman recipe survives today) and were very popular in 18th century Europe. Early 18th century English recipes included boiled custard puddings; a 1750s trifle recipe included boiled custard in the middle. However, during Christmastime today, the words "boiled custard" conjure up a delicious holiday drink that's similar to eggnog but richer and creamier, with no artificial (or real) rum flavoring, cinnamon, or nutmeg. Many people who don't care for eggnog enjoy boiled custard.

Boot

For children in Germany and some other countries the highlight of Advent is December 6. This is known as Nikolaustag or St. Nicholas's Day. Children leave a boot or shoe outside their door on December 5 in anticipation of a visit from Sankt Nikolaus (St. Nicholas). Originally, children left hay or straw for St. Nicholas's horses, but now they leave a boot outside their door or window, or near the fireplace, hoping to find it filled with sweets or chocolates in the morning.

Bowing

A bow was once considered good manners and a gesture of respect. While it is no longer prominent in American culture, it is still prominent in other cultures around the world, particularly in the Orient. A bow can be as simple as lowering the head, or as stately as bending from the waist. It can signify a number of things, including a greeting, a gesture of deference, or an apology.

Bowl Full of Jelly

A bowl full of jelly is the description given to jolly ole Santa's rotund belly in the classic 1800s poem entitled *A Visit from St. Nicholas* but more commonly known as *'Twas the Night Before Christmas.*

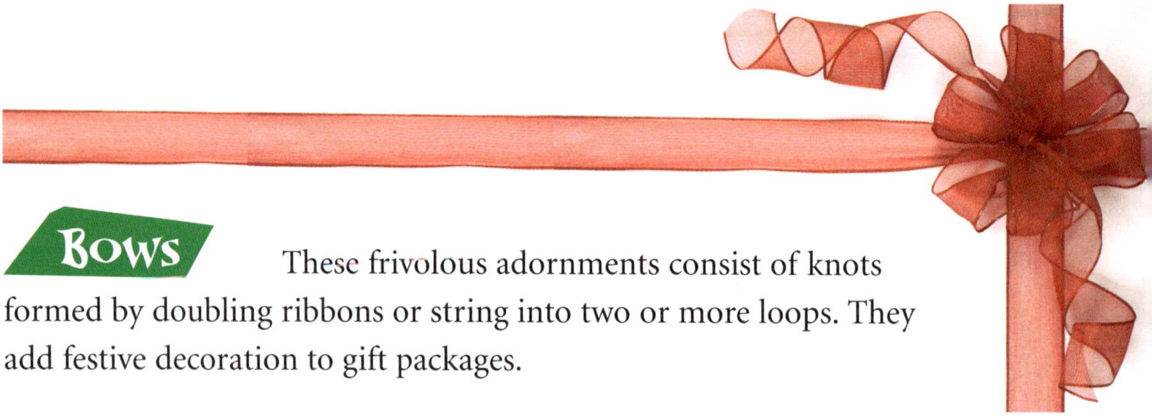

Bows

These frivolous adornments consist of knots formed by doubling ribbons or string into two or more loops. They add festive decoration to gift packages.

Boxing Day

Boxing Day is celebrated in the United Kingdom, Canada, Australia, and New Zealand on December 26. The holiday has nothing to do with the sport of boxing, nor does it have to do with returning unwanted gifts. The origins of Boxing Day can be traced to the practice in Great Britain in earlier times of giving cash or goods to the lower classes (gifts among equals would have already been exchanged on or before Christmas Day). In present day, the custom is to visit relatives, friends, or acquaintances you perhaps have not seen for some time.

Bread

Bread is a staple at mealtime any day of the year, but holiday breads are a Christmas tradition. Many people bake special breads such as pumpkin or banana bread to share with family and friends at holiday mealtimes or to give as gifts. This is especially appropriate at Christmastime, since "bread" is a symbol of the Lord's Presence among His people and "breaking bread" is a sign of fellowship.

Buckeyes

A popular treat during the holiday season, buckeyes are a confection created by dipping peanut butter fudge in milk chocolate and fashioning it to resemble a real buckeye, the brown nut from the buckeye tree.

Bundle of Switches

Children who set out their boot on St. Nicholas's Eve hope for sweets and toys. However, naughty children might receive a bundle of switches (*see* Boot).

Burgermeister Meisterburger

In the 1970 animated classic *Santa Claus Is Comin' to* Town, Herr Burgermeister is the villain. Tiny infant Kris was left on the doorstep of the Kringle family. He grew up wanting to be involved in the Kringle family business of toymaking and delivery of toys to the children of Sombertown. But the town's Burgermeister (Herr Meisterburger), together with an evil wizard named Winter, tries to outlaw toys and prevent Kris's dream from being realized. The voices for this Christmas favorite include Fred Astaire, Mickey Rooney, and Keenan Wynn.

C

Caesar Augustus

See Augustus.

Camel

A large, humped quadraped native to the desert areas of Northern Africa and Asia, the camel was first domesticated over 3,000 years ago. The dromedary camel has a single hump, while the Bactrian camel has two humps. Their average life expectancy is 30 to 50 years. The wise men are often depicted as traveling on camels to visit the Christ Child.

Camel's Hair

In biblical times, hair which was taken from a camel and woven into a coarse cloth. John the Baptist, Jesus' cousin who was born near the same time as Jesus and who was His forerunner, wore a garment made from camel's hair (Matthew 3:4; Mark 1:6). In modern times, camel hair is used to make cloth, painter's brushes, and Oriental rugs.

Candlelight

Candlelight is the warm glow emitted from a burning candle, a reassuring light in the darkness. How fitting that long before we celebrated Christmas, candles represented Christ as the light of the world. People in medieval times believed that the Christ Child wandered the streets on Christmas Eve in search of homes where He would be welcome. Those who hoped He might visit them would light candles and place them in the window as a signal to the Christ Child that He was welcome there. And if someone did come to the door on Christmas Eve, the welcome was assured because the Christ Child might appear as a child; but He also might appear as an old man, a ragged beggar, or in countless other guises. If the homeowner turned away anyone who knocked at the door, the Christ Child in disguise might be the one turned away. So customarily, strangers were welcome. Candles in the windows of our homes and places of worship are a reminder that Christ should be welcome in our hearts and homes, no matter how He chooses to appear.

Candy Cane

It is rumored that the candy cane was invented by French priests in the 1400s and was originally a straight, hard, white stick. Legend has it that in the 1600s, a German choirmaster bent sugar sticks into the shape of a shepherd's staff and gave them out to children attending Christmas services. The holiday custom spread across Europe and eventually to America, where around 1900 the candy cane received its red stripes and peppermint fla-

voring—and the legend of the candy cane was born. Just like the dispute over its origins, there are varying interpretations as to its meaning. The shape of the candy cane is a shepherd's staff, but if turned upside down, it's also a letter "J" for Jesus. Its three smaller red stripes are said to represent the stripes by which we are healed, and the larger red stripe represents Christ's blood shed for us. Some say the peppermint flavor of candy canes is similar to hyssop, which was used during purification rituals by the ancient Israelites. Yet another origin story credits an unknown candy maker who wanted to make a candy in honor of Jesus Christ. In this version, it is said the candy maker wanted the white to represent Jesus' purity, the bold red stripes the crucifixion, and the thin red stripes the Holy Trinity. Whatever the true origin of the candy cane and its intended meaning, it remains an enduring symbol of Christmas.

Cantata

A popular form of chamber music that emerged in the 17th century, the cantata is a choral composition, either sacred or secular. Johann Sebastian Bach composed over 200 cantatas, many of which were for the church.

Cardinal

A beautiful bird found in North America; the male of the species is a bright red. The cardinal frequently adorns Christmas cards, his red coat resplendent against a background of white snow.

Cards, Christmas

The first Christmas card, as we know it, is believed to have been designed in the early 1840s by John Callcott Horsley in England for his friend. The idea caught on, and a first edition of lithographed cards was printed and sold in London. Within 20 years of its first appearance, the Christmas card had become fairly common (*see* Red Suit).

Carol

The origin of the word "carol" goes back to the Greek *choros*, which was the name of a circle dance. The tradition of the Christmas carol dates to the 13th century, with the common people embracing it in the 1400s (at one time, communal expression of the arts was suppressed). A number of carols are based on medieval chord patterns, and religious themes are common; others simply celebrate the holiday season. Many churches hold special Christmas services at which carols are sung.

Caroling

Singing carols, *i.e.*, getting together with a group of people, going outdoors and singing carols, as you move from house to house or place to place. Caroling is one of the older Christmas customs. Some origin stories attribute caroling to St. Francis of Assisi, who led songs of praise in Italy in the 1300s. In England, caroling appears to have its roots in wassailing, a tradition of going from house to house singing, socializing, eating and drinking with friends and relatives, which in earlier times was done during the 12 days of Christmas.

Carrots for Reindeer

Carrots make the perfect snack for Santa's reindeer. A carrot is a root vegetable, which can be eaten raw, boiled, fried, or steamed. Carrots are rich in dietary fiber, antioxidants, and minerals and are a good source of Vitamin A. Too little Vitamin A can result in poor eyesight, so it's always a good idea to eat your carrots. Reindeer love carrots because of their taste. But Santa makes sure to give his reindeer plenty of carrots because he knows that they are a good source of Vitamin A. His reindeer sometimes have to fly through very rough weather conditions, and keen eyesight is crucial for them to stay on course and on schedule.

Caspar

See Magi.

Cattle (lowing)

The cattle of ancient Israel may have looked different from cattle today. A few cattle remain in Israel today and certainly do not resemble the dairy cows with which we are familiar. The term "lowing," as used in the Christmas carol "Away in a Manger," refers to the cattle mooing.

Cave

A cavern or hollow place in the side of a hill; a natural underground chamber. In biblical times, people sometimes took refuge in caves; caves were also frequently used for burial places. Some believe the manger in which Jesus was born was actually in a cave used as a stall for animals. If so, we can derive a tender symbolism from this picture: as Jesus' birth, burial, and resurrection took place in a cave (a hollow place in the heart of the earth), so His birth, death, and resurrection allow us to invite Him to fill the hollow place within our hearts.

Celebration

Commemoration or observation of a day or an event with festivities. We celebrate Christmas on December 25, the traditional date when the birth of Jesus is recognized. This celebration has taken on many traditions and customs such as the Christmas tree, special church services, and the exchange of gifts.

Census

An official counting or registering of citizens. In biblical times, the Romans conducted censuses for the purpose of collecting taxes. Even though Mary was in an advanced stage of pregnancy, she and Joseph were forced to travel to Joseph's ancestral home, Bethlehem, because a census had been ordered. Thus, Jesus was born in Bethlehem, fulfilling the prophecy that the Messiah would be born there (Micah 5:2).

Charity

In the KJV, the word for *love*. Today it has come to mean any act of giving to those in need. The Salvation Army bell ringers, who raise money for charity, have become a familiar sight during the Christmas season (*see* Salvation Army Bell Ringers).

Charlie Brown

Charlie Brown is a character created by Charles M. Schulz in his popular comic strip *Peanuts*. In 1965, an animated film entitled *A Charlie Brown Christmas* made its debut. The story focuses on Charlie Brown's search for the real meaning of Christmas and features Linus, a friend of Charlie's, reciting the birth of Jesus from the Gospel of Luke. *A Charlie Brown Christmas* was a hit, in spite of its low production budget. It remains a timeless Christmas classic, enjoyed by families each holiday season.

Checking It Twice

It has long been rumored that Santa makes a list and checks it twice. People have always believed this to mean that Santa is just being thorough. But perhaps, like many professionals (such as doctors), Santa's handwriting is hurried and hard to read, often causing him to stop and reread his list or enlist the help of an occasional elf to interpret his own writing. Or perhaps, like many of us, Santa just needs better glasses.

Chestnuts

The edible nut of a chestnut tree, immortalized in the opening line of the Mel Torme-Bob Wells' classic "The Christmas Song" as it roasts over an open fire. Roasting chestnuts is a Christmas tradition. A roasted chestnut is sweet and tender; and if you're fortunate enough to live in New York City, these sweet treats are available from street vendors all over the city throughout the Christmas season.

Chex® Mix

Chex® is a family of cereals made by General Mills. In the mid-1950s, the makers of Chex® brand cereal came up with a party mix recipe that instantly became a hit and has remained popular for over 50 years. Although you can now buy ready-made variations of this popular party mix, the recipe for the original Chex® mix can still be found on the company's Web site.

Children

Children need no definition, but perhaps we need to be reminded of just how much Jesus loves them. The Bible tells us how little children were drawn to Jesus. When others tried to push them away, Jesus insisted they be allowed to come to Him. Doing what children do best, they most probably gave Him hugs, climbed into His arms, and sat on His lap. Little children were drawn to the Savior, and He welcomed them with open arms, allowing no one to prevent them from receiving His love and attention. Perhaps we need to remember that we are all the Lord's little children—and He still welcomes us with open arms.

Chimney

While long considered the means by which Santa enters homes on Christmas Eve to leave presents for good little girls and boys, there are many homes without a chimney that, nevertheless, are visited by Santa. Many theories abound as to how Santa actually gets inside a residence, but it remains a mystery.

Chrismon Tree

The word "Chrismon" comes from the Latin *Christi Monogramma*, meaning "monogram of Christ." The origination and development of the Chrismon tree is attributed to Frances Kipps Spencer (1917–1990). In the late 1950s, Mrs. Spencer wanted to find a way to decorate the church Christmas tree in a manner that would be more appropriate for the sanctuary. Ms. Spencer came up with a type of Christmas ornament that reflected the true meaning of Christmas. The symbols used on the ornaments represent a variety of Christian concepts, with designs referencing the life, ministry, and teachings of Jesus Christ. A Chrismon tree is traditionally decked with ornaments of white featuring decorations of gold. As the idea of the Chrismons spread and how-to requests increased, Mrs. Spencer wrote and illustrated five books about Chrismons. She became an active speaker, making tours throughout a number of states to tell the story of her Chrismons.

Christ

Often misunderstood to be a surname of Jesus, the word "Christ" is in fact a title. The English word "Christ" comes from the Greek word *Christos* ("The Anointed One"). *Christos* is a translation of the Hebrew word for "Messiah." "Jesus Christ" is literally "Jesus, the Anointed One." The followers of Jesus are known as Christians because they believe Him to be the Messiah, or the Anointed One, who came in fulfillment of Old Testament prophecies (*see* Jesus Christ).

Christendom

In the broadest sense, Christendom refers to those parts of the world where most people are Christians. It can also refer to the medieval notion of a Christian theocracy (a form of government where God is recognized as the supreme civil ruler). Another meaning is the community of all Christians.

Christmas

From the words "Christ's Mass," Christmas is the annual holiday celebrating the birth of Jesus. The date on which Jesus was born is not actually known (some historians believe it is more likely He was born in April). To most Christians, the fact that He was born is more important than knowing the actual date.

Christmas Cards

See Cards, Christmas.

Christmas Carol, A

See A Christmas Carol.

Christmas Caroling

See Caroling.

Christmas Club

The Christmas Club was a savings program that was offered by most banks during the Great Depression that continued on through the 1970s. The first known Christmas Club was started in 1909 at a bank in Pennsylvania. In later years, the Christmas Club idea became very popular, with banks competing for customers' holiday savings. If you had a Christmas Club account with your local bank, you would routinely make deposits, which you were not allowed to withdraw before Christmas without paying a fee. It was a popular way for families to make certain they had money on hand for the holidays.

Christmas Day

December 25 (*see* Christmas).

Christmas Eve

While this literally means the evening before Christmas or the evening of December 24, it has come to be used for the entire 24-hour period preceding Christmas Day. Christmas Eve is when Santa makes his lightning-fast journey across the globe, leaving gifts for all the good little ones whose names are on his "nice" list (*see* Christmas).

Christmas Eve Communion

A number of Christian denominations hold a special worship service on Christmas Eve during which the congregation is invited to partake of communion, also known as Holy Communion (*see* Eucharist).

Christmas Letter

In our society, where it's all too easy to lose touch with people who are special to us, many folks have adopted the idea of writing a letter to friends and family and either enclosing it in a Christmas card or sending it instead of a Christmas card as their annual Christmas letter. It is a newsy missive filled with all the happenings of the past year along with a wish for the recipient to enjoy a very Merry Christmas.

Christmas Pageants

A Christmas pageant is a play, parade, musical, or some other type of staged presentation performed to celebrate the birth of Jesus. Participating in or attending a Christmas pageant is a great way for children to learn (and adults to be reminded of) what Christmas is really about. Many churches stage children's plays during the Christmas season because it is an enjoyable and effective way to teach children about the story of Jesus' birth and the true meaning of Christmas, not to mention that children always look adorable with halos made of tinsel, fake beards, and wearing their parents' bathrobes.

Christmas Party

A Christmas party can mean the gathering of friends and loved ones to celebrate the Christmas season, or it can denote a semi-obligatory event, such as the office Christmas party. While you might look forward to the family gathering with joyful anticipation, you might look forward to the office party with dread. But, depending on your situation, you may be well advised to smile your way through.

Christmas Play/Program

See Christmas Pageants.

Christmas Shoes

"The Christmas Shoes," a song written by NewSong's Eddie Carswell and Leonard Ahlstrom, is the story of a young boy who wants to buy a pair of new shoes for his dying mother before she meets Jesus. A No. 1 hit for the Christian group NewSong, the song inspired a best-selling book and television film starring Rob Lowe. The poignant story has spread across the Internet in many forms and been attributed to various sources, but the origin appears to be based on a true incident which occurred over a quarter century ago to a woman from Kansas named Helga Schmidt. Ms. Schmidt, who was in a checkout line at Christmas, gave two children $3.00 so they would have enough money to buy a pair of shoes for their mother. She then overheard them say that their mother would be in heaven soon (they wanted her shoes to match the streets of gold). It is said that Ms. Schmidt wrote up the story for her church paper and someone later turned it in to the editors of *Chicken Soup for the Christian Soul* (publisher Health Communications, Inc.), who published it.

Christmas Specials

Christmas specials are a fun part of the holiday season. Almost every TV sitcom features a holiday show, and almost every television channel offers holiday specials—programs filmed just for the holidays, some never before seen, and some that we have watched for decades. Families that once had to search for a single holiday showing of the movie *It's a Wonderful Life* on fuzzy UHF channels can now easily find this holiday favorite. Over the years, some entertainers became known for their wonderful holiday specials. In the 1960s, viewers looked forward to singer Andy Williams's Christmas programs; and Christmas songs he recorded during that period are classics that continue to fill the air waves every Christmas.

Christmas Story, A

See A Christmas Story.

Christmas Tree

The Christmas tree, or Tannenbaum, has become such a popular tradition that it wouldn't seem like Christmas without one. While the traditional Christmas tree is an evergreen, today's Christmas tree can be any color and made from almost any material, from plastic to aluminum. A popular notion embraces the idea that Christmas trees came about thanks to Great Britain's Queen Victoria. However, trees have been decorated to celebrate special occasions for many centuries and by many peoples, including both the Vikings and the Romans. In the Middle Ages, special mystery plays featured a Paradise Tree, which was decorated with apples (representing the forbidden fruit of the Tree of the Knowledge of Good and Evil) and with small white wafers (which represented the Tree of Life). When the mystery plays were suppressed during the 15th century, the Paradise Trees moved from the stage into the home. Britain's Royal Family helped to popularize the custom. In later years, some of the early English Christmas trees were decorated with candles, berries, gingerbread, and fruit. When German immigrants arrived in America, they brought along with them their custom of the Christmas tree, but it wasn't until the 1800s that the Christmas tree was commonly accepted in America. One of the biggest, brightest, most famous Christmas trees of all is the one in Rockefeller Center in New York City, with its 30,000 colored lights. But even if your Christmas tree is more like Charlie Brown's, nothing says Christmas like a Christmas tree (*see* Aluminum).

Christmas Tree Skirt

Christmas trees a couple of centuries ago were decorated by lit candles. A skirt draped around the bottom of the tree would catch the dripping wax. In more modern times, the skirt was perfect for hiding the unsightly but necessary Christmas tree stand. Some Christmas skirts are quite elaborate and much more ornate than the first humble skirts of long ago.

Christmas Truce

On Christmas Eve in 1914, during World War I, something quite remarkable happened. In a region around Belgium, British and German troops squared off. Yet on Christmas Eve, the Germans began decorating the area around their trenches by putting candles on trees and singing Christmas carols. Soon the British troops responded by singing carols of their own. At some point, the soldiers from both sides began calling out Christmas

greetings to one another; eventually, some brave souls even exchanged small gifts with the enemy, such as cigars and chocolate. A brief truce was called so that each side could retrieve fallen comrades and bring them back behind their lines for burial. The truce soon spread to other areas behind the lines. The spontaneous truce did not sit well with some of those in command; and in years to come, artillery bombardments were ordered on Christmas Eve to prevent the repeat of the Christmas Eve truce of 1914.

Christmastide

Christmastide is the festival season (particularly in Great Britain) from Christmas Day to January 5, although the date can vary (in the Roman Catholic Church, the season can begin at the Christmas Vigil Mass and continue until January 13, or even until February 2). This period carries its own customs and observances and is also known as the 12 days of Christmas and Yuletide.

Christos

See Christ; *see also* Jesus Christ.

Cider

Juices pressed from fruits, particularly apples, and used to make a beverage or vinegar. (In modern usage, cider almost always refers to the beverage made from apples.) Cider prior to fermentation is known as sweet cider; after fermentation, it's known as hard cider. In Colonial times, cider was the primary beverage consumed with meals. Hot apple cider is a great wintertime treat, and many people enjoy cider during the Christmas season.

Cinnamon

A common culinary spice made from dried rolled strips of inner bark from any of several East Indian trees. The cinnamon tree also produces an oil, which was used for anointing oil (Exodus 30:23). Cinnamon was once considered a prestigious offering and worthy of presenting to ruling monarchs. Today, cinnamon sticks are often served with hot apple cider, and the ever popular cinnamon roll is the perfect companion for a cup of hot coffee.

Circumcision

A surgical procedure wherein some or all of the foreskin from the male sex organ is removed. Circumcision predates recorded human history and was widely practiced in the ancient world. For the Hebrew people, the rite of circumcision signified their covenant relationship with God. Baby Jesus was circumcised when He was 8 days old (Luke 2:21–24).

City of David

The name given to two cities in the Bible. One was Bethlehem, the ancestral home of David. The other was the city of Jerusalem, which was captured by King David and his men and called the City of David by David himself in 2 Samuel 5:9 (*see* Bethlehem).

Claus, Santa

He is known by many names all over the world: in France, he's Pere Noel; in the United Kingdom, he's Father Christmas; in Italy, he's Babbo Natale; and in the USA, we call him Santa Claus (or simply Santa). Santa Claus is a folklore figure based on the historical figure Saint Nicholas, a bishop from Turkey who supposedly gave presents to the poor. In modern folklore, Santa is a kindly white-haired tubby man who lives at the North Pole, wears a red suit trimmed in white, and brings toys on Christmas Eve to good little boys and girls. Santa has become so identified with Christmas that for some, Santa has supplanted the true meaning of the holiday. For others, however, Santa exists comfortably alongside the true meaning of Christmas, with Christian parents teaching their children that while one is myth, the One whose birth is celebrated on Christmas is real.

Clement Moore

See Moore, Clement C.

Coal

A source of fuel consisting of a black or dark-brown combustible mineral substance; also used to denote burning or charred embers of any kind. The tradition in earlier times of leaving a lump of coal in a stocking for naughty children, instead of the customary nuts, candy, and fruit, is said to have originated in Italy.

Comet

One of Santa's reindeer (*see* Blitzen).

Comfort

To soothe, console, encourage, cheer; a person or thing can also be referred to as a comfort. In 2 Corinthians 1:3, 4, we are encouraged to comfort others as God comforts us (*see* Consolation).

Comfort and Joy

The Christmas carol "God Rest Ye Merry Gentlemen" sings about tidings (news or information) of comfort (*see* Comfort) and joy (great happiness). This refers to the appearance of the angels to the shepherds at the birth of Christ. "And behold, an angel of the Lord stood before them, and the glory of the Lord shone around them, and they were greatly afraid. Then the angel said to them, 'Do not be afraid, for behold, I bring you good tidings of great joy which will be to all people'" (Luke 2:9, 10).

Consolation

To "console" means to alleviate grief, sense of loss, or trouble; to comfort. Jesus is the true source of consolation for Israel, along with the rest of the world. This is what God revealed to Simeon in the Gospel of Luke: "And behold, there was a man in Jerusalem whose name *was* Simeon, and this man *was* just and devout, waiting for the Consolation of Israel, and the Holy Spirit was upon him. And it had been revealed to him by the Holy Spirit that he would

Covenant

An agreement or promise. The Bible refers to God's covenant with Israel, in which God made an agreement with Israel, through Abraham, to protect and take care of His people if they remained obedient and faithful to Him. God also made covenants with Noah and with David. God continues to desire a covenant relationship with people. Through Jesus Christ, God has made a new covenant with humankind; Jesus is referred to in the Book of Hebrews as the mediator of the new covenant (Hebrews 9:15; 12:24).

Cranberries

The fruit of a low creeping shrub or vine, it is initially white but turns a deep red when ripe. Cranberries are made into juice and sauce, among other things. Cranberries have become a traditional part of the American holiday menu. *The Cranberries* are also an alternative Irish rock band, which rose to fame in the 1990s.

Cratchit

Robert "Bob" Cratchit was the unfortunate employee of the miserly Ebenezer Scrooge in Charles Dickens's classic *A Christmas Carol.* Bob Cratchit is a shining example of working "as to the Lord," whether we have a good master or a bad master. In Bob Cratchit's case, he had a bad master. Even though Bob worked in an office where there was so little heat he was cold in winter, and even though his salary was so meager he could barely feed his family, he remained loyal to his employer. Bob had no benefits (there was no health insurance, or even enough money, to obtain medical treatment for Tiny Tim), no 401-K, not even an office Christmas party. There was little to recommend working for Ebenezer Scrooge, except that to be employed by Scrooge was perhaps better than no job at all, though not by much. But Bob suffered this ill treatment with a pure and forgiving heart, and ultimately, he was richly blessed through the very man who had treated him so poorly. Bob Cratchit's forgiving heart was an instrument in the redemption of the soul of another (*see* A Christmas Carol).

Creche

From the French, meaning crib or manger, a creche is a nativity scene, usually depicting the infant Jesus in a manger, surrounded by Mary and Joseph. The scene sometimes includes other figures (the wise men, the shepherds, or angels) and may include animals (camel, sheep, donkey, cow, or others). Some nativity scenes include the Star of Bethlehem. A nativity scene can range from the simple to the elaborate, from the traditional to the unconventional (*see* Drive-Thru Nativity).

Cromwell, Oliver

Oliver Cromwell (1599–1658) was an English political figure and military leader, despised in parts of Ireland to the present day for his ruthless confiscation of Irish land, castles, ancestral homes, and the deportation of families. In the 1640s, the parliamentary party in England prohibited the celebration of Christmas and other holy days, a ban which stayed in effect until the Restoration of 1660. While Oliver Cromwell may not have personally banned Christmas, he is associated with the ban and was quite probably very supportive of it.

Crosby, Bing

There were white Christmases long before Harry Lillis "Bing" Crosby was born in 1903, but it was the combination of Crosby's velvet voice and songwriter Irving Berlin's music and lyrics that gave us one of the most popular Christmas songs of all time. The music and lyrics to "White Christmas" were first written by Irving Berlin in the early 1940s and introduced by Crosby in a 1942 movie called *Holiday Inn*. The song went on to receive the Academy Award for best original song. Bing Crosby's recording was so popular that he sang the song again in a movie musical named after the song, 1954's *White Christmas* starring Bing, Danny Kaye, Rosemary Clooney (George Clooney's aunt), and Vera-Ellen. While Bing Crosby was a legendary singer with a number of hits and a successful film star (particularly noted for his "road" pictures with comedian Bob Hope), he will forever be associated with Christmas.

Cup of Cheer

Dating back to medieval times, a cup of cheer during the Christmas season can mean eggnog, wassail, or hot mulled wine (wine that has been heated with spices added).

Cupid

One of Santa's reindeer (*see* Blitzen).

D

Dancer One of Santa's reindeer (*see* Blitzen).

Dasher One of Santa's reindeer (*see* Blitzen).

David, King David (whose name translates "beloved") is described in the Bible as a man after God's own heart. A young shepherd boy when we first meet him in the Bible, his destiny was to be king of Israel. David was a songwriter (he's one of the primary authors of the Book of Psalms, or songs), a musician, and a dancer (apparently athletic, as the Bible describes him as "leaping and dancing" before the Lord). He was also a military man, a brave and heroic figure. While still a boy tending his father's sheep, he killed both a lion and a bear when they attacked the flock. He was a mere teenager when he killed Goliath, the giant Philistine who had caused the army of Israel to cower in terror. David felled Goliath with a slingshot, trusting in the power of God to be his weapon. David was not a perfect man; many of his mistakes are recorded for us to read. But he was a man

who embraced God with his whole heart. He didn't make excuses for his sins, and he accepted God's punishment of those sins as punishment deserved. It was through the line of David that Jesus Christ came, bringing forgiveness for all humankind.

Day after Thanksgiving Sale

See Black Friday.

Day of the Kings

Traditionally, January 6 (*see* Epiphany).

Dayspring

The dawn, or beginning. Also, Dayspring is a reference to the Messiah as in Luke 1:78, 79: "Through the tender mercy of our God, with which the Dayspring from on high has visited us; to give light to those who sit in darkness and the shadow of death, to guide our feet into the way of peace."

December 25

Christmas Day, a Christian holiday, the day we celebrate the birth of Jesus Christ. It is celebrated in many ways, including the exchange of gifts, special church services, holiday meals, and get-togethers.

Deck the Halls

A Christmas carol, whose origin is unknown but widely believed to be Welsh, circa 16th or 17th century. It resembles songs of the English Renaissance, particularly the madrigals that were in fashion during

that period. It is known that Mozart (1756–1791) used the tune in a violin-piano duet. Whatever its origin, it is a festive, enduring Christmas carol and a timeless expression of the joy of the Christmas season (*see* Apparel).

Decree

A proclamation, official order, or command issued by a king or ruling monarch. It was actually Caesar Augustus's census decree that set the Christmas story in motion because it forced Joseph and Mary to return to Bethlehem, the place where their Son Jesus had been prophesied to be born (Luke 2:1).

Deity

Someone who is divine; the Supreme Being; God. Jesus Christ was born a human baby; however, He retained His deity and was both fully God and fully man.

Department Store Santa

Explained away by many parents to their offspring as "Santa's helpers" (except for those who try to pass him off as the real deal), the department store Santa first appeared on the scene in 1841 when a Philadelphia merchant named Parkinson hired a man to dress up in a Kris Kringle outfit and climb the chimney of his store. Forty years later the Boston Store in Brockton, Massachusetts, hired a Scottish immigrant to pose as Santa Claus. The idea of the department store Santa became popular, soon spreading to other countries. The early department store Santas would hardly recognize the modern-day department store Santa. Today's Santa is often found in shopping malls surrounded by ornate trappings, Santa's helpers, and a photographer, not to mention the large numbers of children, just like Ralphie Parker, who line up to whisper their secret wishes in Santa's ear (*see* A Christmas Story).

Diamonds

A pure (or nearly pure) extremely hard form of carbon, which when cut and polished, makes a precious gem and something that any mommy would love to get as a present under the tree. Diamonds are a symbol of love and in Western culture, they are the traditional gem for an engagement ring.

Dirty Santa

A popular game played during the Christmas season where each guest brings a wrapped gift (usually there's a set limit on how much you can spend for the gift) with no identifying tags. The gift is placed under a tree with everyone else's gift. Numbers are drawn and turns taken numerically. When one's number is called, a gift may be taken from under the tree or stolen from an earlier player. The higher your number, the better choice you have.

Disciples

Students, pupils, or followers. The closest 12 of Jesus' original followers are often referred to as the 12 disciples.

Discount

What every shopper hopes to receive at Christmastime while doing their Christmas shopping; the bigger the discount, the better. A discount is also often the justification for impulse purchases and buyer's remorse.

Trivia

Amy Grant's song "Tennessee Christmas" was recorded in which state?

a. California—she was missing home, though.
b. Tennessee—duh!
c. Colorado—she refers to it in the song.
d. Trick question—it was recorded in Saskatchewan!

Answer: C. "Tennessee Christmas" was recorded at a ranch in Nederland, Colorado.

Divinity

The quality or state of being divine, often used to refer to the attributes of God.

Divinity is also a type of candy often served during the Christmas season. Recipes for divinity candy can be found in cookbooks or online; and a basic recipe might include sugar, corn syrup, walnuts, egg whites, and vanilla, among other ingredients.

Donkey

One of the animals found in the Bible, a domestic beast of burden, most probably originating in Africa. Jesus' mother Mary is often shown riding a donkey to Bethlehem, although no donkey is actually mentioned in the Bible's accounts of Jesus' birth.

Donner

One of Santa's reindeer (*see* Blitzen).

Dove

One of the animals of the Bible, a pure white bird that may represent innocence, gentleness, love, and purity; a symbol of the Holy Spirit. Artwork depicting a dove often graces the front of Christmas cards, or the dove's likeness may be fashioned into Christmas tree ornaments.

Dreams

A succession of images, thoughts, and scenes that occur while sleeping. In ancient times, dreams were believed to convey messages from God (Genesis 31:10–13; Numbers 12:6; Matthew 1:20); and to be able to interpret dreams, as Joseph in the Old Testament did, was considered a gift from God. In the case of Joseph, his ability to interpret dreams landed him a position as the second most powerful man in Egypt, second only to Pharaoh himself. In the New Testament, Jesus' stepfather, also named Joseph, was warned by God that Herod wanted to kill the boy Jesus. Because Joseph understood and obeyed the dream, he and his family escaped Herod's wrath (*see* Egypt).

Drifts

A snowdrift is a deposit of snow created during snowstorms. Some can be small, some can be sizeable, and some of them provide quite a challenge to Dad and his shovel.

Drive-thru Nativity

Many churches host outdoor living nativity scenes each year where church members dress up as Joseph, Mary, the baby Jesus, shepherds, and wise men. More elaborate scenes use live animals such as sheep and donkeys; and some even include more unusual animals like camels. Drive-thru nativities are especially designed so that visitors can simply drive through the nativity scene without having to leave the comfort and warmth of their cars (*see* Creche).

Drummer Boy

"Little Drummer Boy" is such a popular Christmas carol that it's difficult to believe it's only been around since 1958. It's been recorded a countless number of times and was Bing Crosby's second most successful recording following "White Christmas" (*see* Bing Crosby). In 1968, an animated Christmas special of the song was produced by Rankin-Bass and is shown each Christmas, along with other animated classics of the holiday season.

Drummers

People who play the drums. Drums figure prominently in holiday music and holiday themes, from "Little Drummer Boy" to *The Nutcracker Ballet.*

E

Ebenezer

"Ebenezer" means "Stone of Help." It is mentioned in the Bible as the scene of a battle between the Israelites and the Philistines and is also the name given to the stone marker erected at the site. In modern terminology, many Christians consider an Ebenezer to be a milestone that marks an important part of their journey; or spiritually, it may be anything that reminds us of God's help, His love, or His presence. In a secular sense, the name "Ebenezer" is most often associated with Ebenezer Scrooge (*see* A Christmas Carol; *see also* Ebenezer Scrooge).

Ebenezer Scrooge

The main character in Charles Dickens's 1843 novel *A Christmas Carol*. The story of Ebenezer Scrooge is the story of the redemption of a man's life and the transformation of a cold, uncaring, bitter, miserly, selfish, friendless man into a generous, caring, faithful friend. The surname "Scrooge" has come to mean a penny-pinching miser (*see* A Christmas Carol).

Eggnog

Eggnog is a drink made of milk or cream, eggs, sugar (wine or rum optional). Other ingredients are spices such as nutmeg, cinnamon, or allspice. Eggnog is associated with the holidays, specifically with Christmas and New Year's. Commercial nonalcoholic eggnog is available during the holidays at many grocery stores. It is believed that the eggnog tradition began in Europe in the 17th century when it was served at social gatherings. Eggnog was brought to America by the Colonists, who added rum, a cheap liquor imported from the Caribbean. Eggnog soon became a favorite holiday drink in America and remains so to this day. Some who prefer a milder form of holiday beverage choose boiled custard instead (*see* Boiled Custard).

Egypt

The Egyptian Nile Valley is home to one of the oldest cultures in the world, spanning three thousand years of continuous history. Ancient Egypt was among the earliest civilizations; and for millennia, Egypt maintained a strikingly complex and stable culture that influenced later cultures of Europe, the Middle East, and Africa. Egypt figures prominently in the Bible. It is where Joseph was taken into captivity and where he became the second most powerful man in the land, second only to Pharaoh himself. God used Joseph's position to save his family and the nation of Israel itself during seven years of drought

and famine. Egypt was once again a sanctuary many years later when another Joseph had to flee Israel with his wife Mary and the infant Jesus, whom Herod was seeking to kill. An angel of the Lord appeared in a dream to Jesus' stepfather Joseph and urged him to take the child to Egypt. There the family remained until the death of Herod, which fulfilled the prophecy, "Out of Egypt I called My Son" (Matthew 2:13–15).

Elf

A mythical creature, not quite as tall as human beings, with pointed ears. Elves are said to inhabit forests and springs, and a fortunate few live at the North Pole, where they work as assistants to Santa in his workshop, helping him make toys to deliver on Christmas Eve to good little girls and boys.

Elizabeth

Elizabeth was the mother of John the Baptist. She was the wife of a priest named Zacharias and first cousin to Mary, the mother of Jesus. Elizabeth waited many years to have a child and was thought to be barren. But God heard Elizabeth and Zacharias's prayers and sent her a very special son, the prophet John. He was one of the greatest prophets the world has seen and the messenger who ushered in the Messiah.

Emmanuel

See Immanuel.

Epiphany

An epiphany is the sudden comprehension or realization of the meaning of something (*to have an epiphany*). It is also the name given to the Christian feast that celebrates the revelation of God to humankind in human form. Epiphany is traditionally celebrated on January 6 and marks the day the magi (wise men) came seeking the infant Jesus and who, on finding Him, recognized He was the Christ.

Eternal Life

Promised to all who believe in Jesus Christ, eternal life is not only a life promised to us in the future, after death, but the apostle John declares that Christians have already begun to experience eternal life because they have a relationship with God and with His Son, Jesus Christ (John 17:3).

Eucharist

The sacrament of Holy Communion, the Lord's Supper; the consecrated elements of the Communion, especially the bread (*see* Christmas Eve Communion).

Evergreen

A type of tree, also known as a conifer because of the cones that hold its seeds. Evergreens have foliage that remains green through more than one growing season; and they thrive in cold climates, surviving where there is little sunshine and little available water. Evergreens make popular Christmas trees (*see* Christmas Tree).

Evil

The opposite of good; a force that opposes God and the people of God (Romans 7:8–19).

Trivia

Reindeer are actually . . .

a. Mythological creatures created by Christmas card companies.
b. Elk.
c. Delicious.
d. Caribou.

Answer: D. Reindeer are actually wild caribou.

Exultation

Lively or triumphant joy; to be extremely joyful, an exuberant expression of such joy. The Christmas carol "O Come All Ye Faithful" urges choirs of angels to "sing in exultation" to celebrate the birth of Jesus.

F

Fa la la la la From “Deck the Halls,” a Christmas carol (*see* Deck the Halls; *see also* Apparel).

Factory A manufacturing facility—Santa’s real workshop.

Faith Faith is a very real and powerful force, and it is extremely important to God (God says that without faith, it is impossible to please Him). Many erroneously think that faith lives in the feelings or emotions, but the seat of faith in human beings is in the spirit, the part of us closest to God. Faith can transform lives and bring about miracles; the Bible tells us it is the substance of things hoped for, the evidence of things unseen. Jesus did not walk upon water;

water can't support a human's weight. Jesus walked on faith, which held Him up as He crossed deep waters. His life is an example of unwavering faith. Faith is so important to God that God counted Abraham's faith as righteousness. Faith is one of the gifts of the Holy Spirit, given by the One who is the author and finisher of our faith (Hebrews 12:2).

Family A group of persons, generally related by blood or marriage, who form a household. Many Christians refer to other Christians with whom they fellowship as their "church family" and feel as close to them as if they were related by blood.

Father Christmas *See* Claus, Santa.

Favorite Things A song, "My Favorite Things" by Richard Rodgers and Oscar Hammerstein was performed in the hit musical *The Sound of Music.*

Feliz Navidad "Merry Christmas" in Spanish. The song "Feliz Navidad" was recorded by Jose Feliciano in the 1970s and became such a popular Christmas song that many think Christmas would just not be Christmas without hearing it.

Fiber Optic Lights

Fiber optic is a technology developed in the late 1950s but only recently found in wide usage. In this technology, light is passed along glass or plastic threads. A point of light is visible at the end of the thread; and, when grouped with many strands of thread, a delicate spray of light is produced. Many indoor artificial trees come prestrung with lights, and others are lit by fiber optics.

Fir

An evergreen tree. The fir tree is mentioned several times in the Bible; the Israelites used it for making musical instruments, for building ships, and for building the temple. It is also a biblical symbol, which represents the blessing of God (Isaiah 41:19; 55:13).

Fire

The process of combustion in which material is ignited, giving off heat and flames; a burning mass of material; the thing Santa doesn't want to see when he comes down the chimney.

Five Golden Rings

From the song *The Twelve Days of Christmas* (*see* Twelve Days of Christmas).

Flake

A particle of snow. God pays enough attention to the details to make sure that no two snowflakes are ever the same. If He cares that much about snowflakes, how must He feel about you?

Flesh

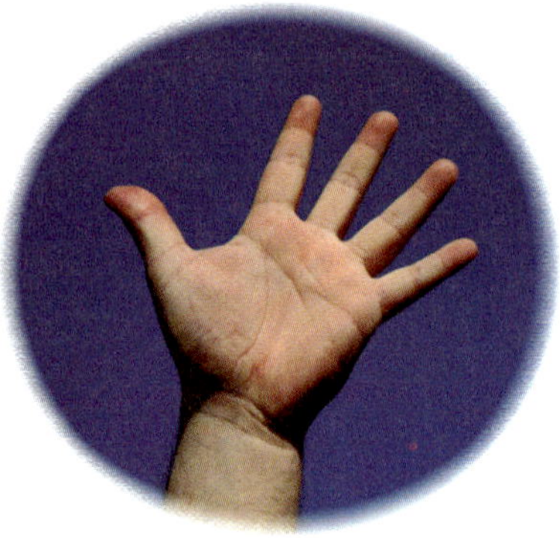

The physical bodies of humans or animals, consisting of muscle and fat. Jesus was born into our world with a fleshly body like ours.

Flurries

Brief, light, intermittent snow showers.

Forgiveness

The act of excusing an offense; to pardon. Because of Jesus' birth, death, and resurrection, we have received pardon, or forgiveness, for our sins. If Jesus had not been born, there would be no forgiveness for our offenses against God.

Fourth Friday in November

See Black Friday.

Frankincense

Used chiefly in incense and perfumes, it is an aromatic gum resin from African and Asian trees. One of the gifts brought to the infant Jesus by the wise men (*see* Magi).

Friday after Thanksgiving

See Black Friday.

Friday, Black

See Black Friday.

Friends

A person attached to another by warm feelings of personal regard and trust. According to Scripture, Jesus calls us His friends if we obey Him (John 15:14).

Frosty the Snowman

A popular Christmas song, which was recorded by Gene Autry in 1950, following his hit record *Rudolph the Red-Nosed Reindeer*. "Frosty the Snowman" was made into an animated short first in 1954 and again in 1969—the latter by Rankin-Bass. The Rankin-Bass animated tale has become a Christmas classic and is aired each year during the Christmas season (*see* Happy Birthday!!).

Fruit Baskets for Shut-ins

A shut-in is someone who is confined to home, a hospital, or nursing home due to illness, frailty, or infirmity. Some churches, benevolent organizations, and caring individuals take fruit baskets to shut-ins during the holidays.

Trivia

Which is the original lyric? "Have yourself a merry little Christmas . . .

a. . . . it may be your last, next year we may all be living in the past."
b. . . . let your heart be light, from now on our troubles will be out of sight."
c. . . . make your yuletide gay, from now on our troubles will be miles away."
d. . . . trim the Christmas tree, say a little prayer for you and me."

Answer: A. It underwent many revisions because folks found it depressing.

Fruitcake

The fruitcake dates back as far as Roman times. During the Middle Ages, crusaders reportedly carried this type of cake to sustain themselves for long periods of time away from home. During the 1400s, the British began making fruitcake with dried fruits from the Mediterranean. In the early 18th century, fruitcakes (also called plum cakes) were outlawed throughout Continental Europe (they were considered sinfully rich). By the end of the 18th century, there were laws restricting the use of plum cakes. At the turn of the century, fruitcakes were extremely popular and no longer illegal or restricted. In modern times, the fruitcake is not accorded the respect it once knew. Fruitcake is considered a less than desirable gift by many, yet others look forward to the Christmas season and feel that it wouldn't be the same without fruitcake.

Fudge

A soft candy made of chocolate, sugar, milk, and butter. There are many variations, such as peanut butter fudge and walnut fudge, among others.

Future, Ghost of Christmas

One of the three ghosts (Christmas Past, Christmas Present, and Christmas Future) who visit Ebenezer Scrooge (*see* A Christmas Carol).

Trivia

These are all traditional Christmas stories except:

a. *The Old Curiosity Shop*
b. *The Cricket and the Hearth*
c. *The Gift of the Magi*
d. *The Fir Tree*

Answer: A. *The Old Curiosity Shop* was Charles Dickens's tale of poverty in London.

Gabriel An archangel who is a messenger from God (Daniel 8:16; Luke 1:19, 26–38). Christian tradition holds that Gabriel is the angel who will usher in the final judgment by blowing his trumpet.

Galilee A province that was the home of Jesus for most of His life. The villages of Nazareth and Capernaum were both in Galilee.

Gift Card Gift cards have increased in popularity, primarily for two reasons: (1) their convenience, and (2) the recipient has a hand in selecting his/her own gift. A gift card is purchased from a retailer or bank in a specified amount, which the purchaser prepays; the card is then given to the recipient, who can redeem it for the amount credited to the card. Gift cards are available for almost everything, from restaurants to shopping malls and even Internet shopping.

Gift Certificate

The forerunner of the gift card, only in the form of a certificate (*see* Gift Card).

Gift Giving

To give someone a present, frequently an exchange of gifts. When Jesus was born, wise men brought the infant gifts, which consisted of gold, frankincense, and myrrh (*see* Magi).

Trivia

The historical Saint Nicholas is legendary for:

a. His striking white beard, which he trimmed at Winter's end.
b. Instituting a Christmas feast at which everyone wore red or white.
c. Sneaking money or gifts to the poor.
d. Hanging socks on the mantle for the wise men to fill with presents.

Answer: C. Saint Nicholas is also the patron saint of sailors.

Gift of the Magi

A classic short story by O. Henry (the pen name for novelist William S. Porter, 1862–1910) in which a wife sells her beautiful knee-length hair to buy a fob for her husband's watch, and her husband sells his treasured watch to buy combs for his wife's hair.

Gimbels

Gimbels was a department store founded in the 1880s in Milwaukee, Wisconsin. In 1894, the Gimbels opened another store in Philadelphia; in 1910, another followed in New York City. Gimbels was a rival to Macy's Department Store (Gimbels was once directly across from Macy's on 34th street in New York City). The famous rivalry between the two stores was featured in the film *Miracle on 34th Street*. Macy's is still in existence, but the last Gimbels store closed in 1987.

Gingerbread

Gingerbread dates back to ancient times. In 2000 B.C., wealthy Greek families traveled to the Isle of Rhodes to buy spiced honey cakes. In the 11th century, crusaders brought back with them the spices and other ingredients that became essential for making gingerbread. Around the 1300s, the English added bread crumbs. The bread was often stale, and the spices tended to be heavy to disguise this fact, which led to the distinctive taste of gingerbread. Gingerbread was so popular during medieval times that the people held festivities known as gingerbread fairs. The popularity of gingerbread spread; and eventually, Nuremberg, Germany, became known as the gingerbread capital of the world. Nuremberg gingerbread was not baked at home; it was made exclusively by a group of master bakers known as the *Lebkuchler,* who made gingerbread in many

shapes and sizes, including angels, wreaths, and hearts. Today, gingerbread hearts are offered year-round at German festivals, and larger pieces of gingerbread are used to make gingerbread houses.

Gingerbread Houses

Miniature edible houses made of gingerbread and decorated with icing, colored sugar, and candy. These are predominately for decoration and are particularly popular at Christmastime (*see* Gingerbread).

Glitter

To glisten or sparkle brilliantly. Glitter, as we know it, is tiny squares of metallic plastic used by adults and children alike. Glue is placed in the desired pattern on everything from homemade Christmas cards to felt stockings, and glitter is liberally applied. Unfortunately, the application usually includes the floor, body parts, and innocent bystanders.

Gloria in Excelsis Deo

Latin for "Glory to God in the Highest." The Gloria is a hymn of praise addressed to each Person of the Holy Trinity. This is the refrain of one of the most beloved Christmas carols, "Angels We Have Heard on High."

Glory

To give glory to God is to give worshipful praise and thanksgiving. Glory is also used to describe God's beauty, power, and perfection—the wondrous aura of His presence. In the New Testament, the glory of God is reflected mainly in the Person of Jesus Christ (Luke 9:29–32; John 2:11). Christ now shares His glory with His church, as we are transformed into His glorious image (John 17:5, 6, 22; 2 Corinthians 3:18).

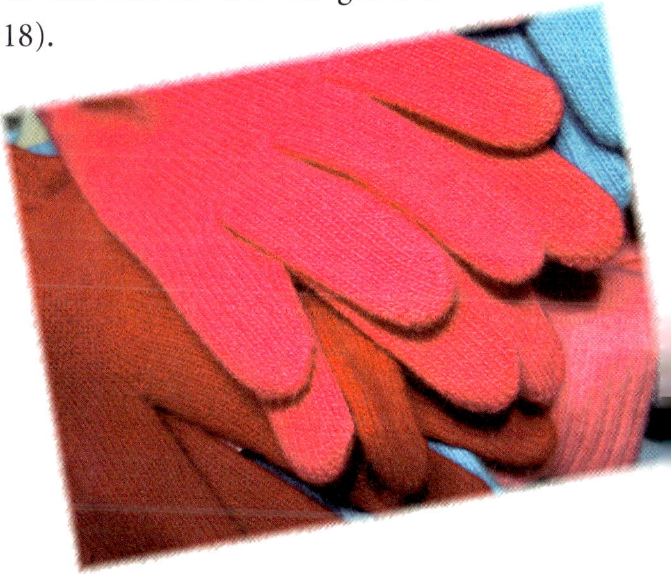

Glove

A covering for the hand made with a place for each finger and thumb. Gloves keep hands from turning into popsicles during the cold winter months!

God

God is a mystery. That doesn't mean that He cannot be known; it simply means that He can never be fully understood. Because He is Spirit, He is invisible. Because He is perfect, He does not change, nor will He ever die. He is also all-knowing, all-powerful, and ever-present. That means He knows everything, He can do anything, and He is everywhere. No matter where we are or what we need, He can find us and help us. Furthermore, God is holy, righteous, loving, truthful, and wise. So we know that He will always do the right thing, even when we don't know what that would be.

Even though God is beyond our comprehension and we can never fully understand Him, He wants everyone to know Him. That's why He has taken great pains to reveal Himself to everyone. God is the Creator of the universe and is therefore revealed through the natural world around us. He is the Father of Jesus

Christ and is therefore revealed even more perfectly through His Son. He also inspired the writings of the Bible, which records revelations of Him throughout history, through creation, and through the life of His Son, Jesus. Therefore, for many people looking for God, the beginning point is simply reading the Bible.

God Bless Us Everyone

The phrase uttered by Tiny Tim in Charles Dickens's *A Christmas Carol* (*see* A Christmas Carol).

Godhead

The Godhead is comprised of God the Father, Jesus His Son, and the Holy Spirit—distinct Persons, but still "one." The word "Godhead" appears in the famous Christmas carol "Hark the Herald Angels Sing":

Veiled in flesh the Godhead see;
Hail the incarnate Deity,
Pleased as man with man to dwell,
Jesus, our Emmanuel.
Hark! The herald angels sing,
"Glory to the newborn King!"

For more on the individual members of the Godhead, see the entries for "God," "Holy Spirit," and "Jesus."

Gold

A precious metallic element, yellow in color, not subject to corrosion. One of the gifts brought to the infant Jesus by the wise men (*see* Magi).

Good News

In biblical terms, the Gospel of Jesus Christ. The Good News is that Jesus is the Son of God, that He died for our sins, and that He was raised from the dead in order to offer eternal life to any who have the faith to follow Him.

Good Tidings

Good news. When the angels appeared to the shepherds to announce the birth of Jesus, they said they were bringing "good tidings of great joy which will be to all people" (Luke 2:10).

Goodwill

Benevolence or kindness; a friendly disposition. At the birth of the Savior, God sent heavenly messengers to announce peace on Earth, goodwill toward men, evidencing His willingness to embrace us.

Trivia

Which of the following artists has never recorded "Silent Night"?

a. The Brady Bunch
b. Christina Aguilera
c. Five For Fighting
d. Cyndi Lauper

Goodwill Toward Men

See Goodwill.

Gospels

The first four books of the New Testament—Matthew, Mark, Luke, and John—are known as the "Gospels." They tell the story of the life of Jesus Christ. Even though all of the Gospels tell essentially the same story, each one is unique and shows us different insights into the life and teachings of Jesus. Taken together, they help form a more complete picture of who He is and what He did. The word "gospel" literally means "good news." The Gospels proclaim the good news of Jesus Christ.

Answer: B. All the other artists have recorded some form of "Silent Night."

Governor

A ruler of a state, town, or province.

Grace

As used in the Bible, God's favor or goodwill (*see* Goodwill).

Gracious

See Grace.

Grandma Got Run over by a Reindeer

A humorous Christmas song, written by Randy Brooks in the 1970s and recorded by the husband/wife duo Elmo and Patsy, it tells the story of how Grandma had too much Christmas cheer (eggnog), decided to go home to retrieve her medication, and got run over by a reindeer, which killed her. Grandma's Christmas may have been ruined by the reindeer, but the flying assassin has brought a lot of laughter to the rest of us.

Green

The second color of Christmas (the first being red), green signifies life—in particular, the hope of eternal life, which Jesus Christ offers.

Greensleeves

A traditional English folk song. The song is commonly associated with Anne Boleyn due to the legend that King Henry VIII of England (1491–1547) composed the song for Anne, his future queen. The tune has been adopted by the beautiful Christmas carol "What Child Is This?"

Greetings

The act or words of someone who greets someone else. It has come to mean the expressed hope of well-being for another.

Grinch

Someone who spoils things for others; a grouch. The word originated from the name of a character created by Dr. Seuss (Theodor Seuss Geisel). The Grinch appeared in Seuss's 1957 book *How the Grinch Stole Christmas*. The book caught on and became so popular that in 1966 an animated television special was produced. It was so well received that it continues to be aired during the Christmas holidays. Although the Grinch appeared in other Dr. Seuss stories, he is forever identified with Christmas. The large mean green Grinch was memorably portrayed by actor Jim Carrey in a 2000 film directed by Ron Howard.

Gumdrops

Small chewy candy made of sweetened gum or gelatin and coated with sugar. Gumdrops are often used to decorate gingerbread houses, popular at Christmastime.

Hallelujah Chorus from the Messiah A chorus from an oratorio by George Frideric Handel (*see* Handel).

Handel George Frideric Handel (1685–1759), a German-born composer who lived most of his life in England and eventually became a subject of the British crown. His most famous work is *Messiah*, an oratorio that draws on texts taken from the King James Bible.

Handel's Messiah *See* Handel.

Hanukkah Also *Hanukah* or *Chanukah*, an eight-day Jewish holiday that celebrates the rededication of the temple in Jerusalem in 165 B.C.; also called *Feast of Dedication* or *Festival of Lights*. It is celebrated in the Hebrew month of Chislev, which usually occurs in mid to late December, and includes lighting the eight candles of a menorah (*see* Menorah).

Happy Birthday!!

From the animated 1969 *Frosty the Snowman*. When a magic silk top hat is placed on the head of Frosty the Snowman, he comes to life and shouts, "Happy Birthday!!" (*See* Frosty the Snowman.)

Hark

Listen! A word rarely used today, we recognize it most readily from the Christmas carol "Hark, the Herald Angels Sing."

Hay

Cut and dried grass, used for fodder. This is what the infant Jesus probably lay upon in the manger on the night of His birth.

Hell

"Hell" describes the afterlife of suffering caused by sin. Many Christians believe that hell is an actual place. Others believe that it is a term that simply describes the condition of a soul that is eternally separated from God. Either way, one thing is for sure: Jesus came to save us from hell. By believing that Jesus is the Son of God and by following Him as our Lord, hell holds no more threat for us.

Herald A royal or official messenger, such as a herald angel. These are the angels that appeared to the shepherds and announced the birth of Jesus.

Herod There were actually several Roman rulers named "Herod" in the Bible. The first Herod mentioned in the Bible reigned under the Roman government as the king of all Judea. He felt threatened when he heard the prophecy that the Messiah, the "King of the Jews," had been born, so he had all the male infants born in the region of Bethlehem slaughtered in order to protect his own throne. But God helped Joseph and Mary escape to Egypt with Jesus. They were able to hide there until Herod died. However, another Herod was on the throne during the time of Jesus' ministry. He was the one who imprisoned John the Baptist and allowed him to be beheaded. Later, when Jesus had been arrested, he turned Jesus' fate over to Pontius Pilate (*see* Pontius Pilate).

Ho! Ho! Ho! Santa's distinctive laugh.

Holiday Originally this word was "holy day." Today, it is a day observed, by law or by custom, to commemorate a special event; frequently, a day on which some businesses are closed and on which you don't have to go to work or to school; a special day in which the normal routine is temporarily suspended.

Holiday Inn

A 1942 movie starring Bing Crosby, Fred Astaire, and Marjorie Reynolds, *Holiday Inn* introduced the Christmas song "White Christmas." In the movie, the Holiday Inn was an inn that opened only on public holidays. The hotel chain named Holiday Inn, which was founded in 1952 in Memphis, Tennessee, was actually named after the fictional Holiday Inn from the movie.

Holly

Holly includes around 400 species of trees and shrubs, among which is the American Holly (the state tree of Delaware). The foliage and berries of holly plants are used for decoration, especially at Christmastime.

Holly and the Ivy

A Christmas carol, which dates back at least to the 1700s but which may be much older, since the praise of the holly and the ivy was a favorite subject among medieval carolers.

Holly Jolly

From "Holly Jolly Christmas," written by Johnny Marks (the composer of "Rudolph the Red-Nosed Reindeer") and first recorded by the Quinto Sisters in 1962. The version of the song that is most remembered, however, is the later recording by Burl Ives, an established folk singer and actor; it became his signature song.

Holy

To be holy means to be good, righteous, whole, and complete. God is holy, and anyone or anything that is set apart for God is declared holy by God. Of course, no one in this world can ever be truly holy. However, once a person decides to follow God, God begins the process of making that person more like Himself, making him or her holy. This process ends when God's people join Him in eternity. Once they see God, they will finally be complete.

Holy Spirit

The Holy Spirit is the third Person of the Holy Trinity. He is the One who exercises God's power in the world and makes faith possible. No one can come to the Father except through the Son, but it is only through the Holy Spirit that we have the revelation of Jesus as the Son of God. In fact, the primary ministry of the Holy Spirit is to bring glory to the Father and the Son. That is one reason why the Father and the Son often seem more prominent than the Holy Spirit in the Scriptures: the Holy Spirit inspired the writers of the Bible, and the Holy Spirit delights in revealing the Father and the Son.

Although the Holy Spirit is often represented through symbols such as a flame or a dove, it is important that we understand that He is just as much a Person as are the other members of the Trinity—not an "it," not a thing. Since He is the expressed power of the Trinity who reveals God to us, it is of utmost importance that we do not grieve Him. In fact, we should appeal to the Holy Spirit to make His dwelling among us because "Now the Lord is the Spirit; and where the Spirit of the Lord *is,* there *is* liberty" (2 Corinthians 3:17).

Home for the Holidays

The place we all long to be at Christmastime. "(There's No Place Like) Home for the Holidays" by Robert Allen and Al Stillman is a sentimental favorite.

Hope

To look forward to; to anticipate with confidence or desire.

Horse

A large quadruped; an animal that has been domesticated since ancient times. The most popular horse at Christmastime is the hobby horse or rocking horse. The earliest rocking horses most likely originated in Germany circa 1700.

Hosanna

A shout of exclamation or praise to God.

Host

The consecrated wafer or bread of the Eucharist (*see* Eucharist); also, a person who entertains guests in his home.

Hot Apple Cider

See Cider.

Hot Chocolate

Hot chocolate dates back to ancient times. Mayan Indians harvested cocoa beans, which they ground and mixed with water and spices to form the drink xocoatl. The explorer Cortez established a cocoa plantation in Mexico in the early 1500s, and it is Cortez who is credited with introducing the drink to Europeans. In the early 1600s, the *chocolat* drink became popular among French aristocracy, and a Frenchman opened the first cafe specializing in *chocolat* in London in 1657. In April 1828, a Dutchman named Van Houten patented a process to extract the natural fat from the bean, known as cocoa butter, and the chocolate bar was born. Cocoa is still sometimes referred to as Dutch chocolate.

Hot Cocoa

See Hot Chocolate.

Hot Toddy

A drink consisting of liquor, sugar, spices, and hot water.

Trivia

It's a Wonderful Life is set in:

a. Bedford Falls
b. Chippewa Falls
c. Chippewa Plains
d. Niagara Falls

Answer: A. The setting is a small, quaint U.S. town.

I

Icicles Frozen spikes of tapered ice formed by frozen dripping or falling water.

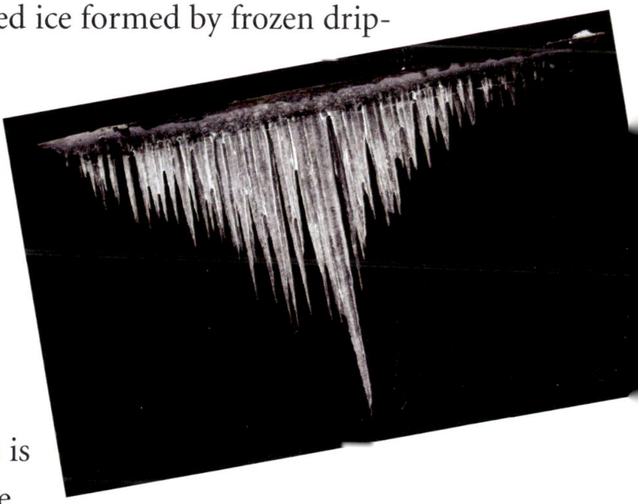

Immanuel Also spelled "Emmanuel," it means "God with Us." It is the name used by the prophet Isaiah in referring to the Messiah and is one of the names of Jesus Christ (Matthew 1:23), who is Immanuel come to ransom not only captive Israel, but all of humankind.

Immortality Life eternal, unending life. The Israelites believed in the survival of the spirit after death, as do Christians today. Jesus spoke of both the "resurrection of life" and the "resurrection of condemnation," so it appears that both believers and nonbelievers will be resurrected, but their eternal destinies will not be the same.

Incarnate

To incarnate means to give something a bodily form. For instance, in the Bible, Satan is incarnated as a serpent. But Christ, the Son of God, is incarnated as a servant and a sacrifice.

Incarnation

The term "Incarnation" isn't used in the Bible itself. However, scholars of the Bible use this word to describe the coming of God's Son, Jesus Christ, into the world as a human being. Jesus took all of His divinity and poured it into a mortal form in order to save all of humanity. He experienced all the pain of living as a human being in a fallen world. He endured grief, suffering, torture, punishment, and even a grueling death for our sakes. Because of living life as one of us, He has sympathy and empathy for all of us. And because He suffered and died for all, eternal life is now available to each of us. If we simply believe and follow Jesus, He will lead us throughout our lives in this fallen world until we inherit eternal life with Him in a perfect world.

Trivia

According to the Gospels, what were the names of the three wise men?

a. Alvin, Simon, and Theodore
b. Kaspar, Melchior, and Balthasar
c. Peter, Paul, and Mary
d. The Gospels do not list the wise men's names

Answer: D. The Gospels do not list their names, whether they were kings, or if there were three of them.

Incense

A substance that produces a sweet odor when burned, used in religious ceremonies or to enhance a mood by filling the air with a sweet aroma. Incense was burned as an offering to God and symbolized the prayers of the Hebrew people, which were pleasing to God.

Inn

In biblical times, hospitality was considered a duty. Most travelers lodged in private residences. An inn was not necessarily what we would imagine today; the lodgings in an inn were often primitive shelters for travelers and their animals. Inns were built along trade routes, just as you see motels built along busy highways today. Joseph and Mary were turned away from an inn by the innkeeper, in spite of Mary's advanced state of pregnancy (*see* Innkeeper).

Innkeeper

One who manages or runs an inn (*see* Inn).

Isaiah

Isaiah was one of the writers of the Old Testament. He was a prophet who wrote about the coming of the Messiah, Jesus Christ, in a book we now refer to as "Isaiah." The book deals with God's upcoming judgment upon Israel and a future outpouring of grace and mercy to them as well. God gave Isaiah revelations so that He could prepare His people for the coming judgment, even

though He knew that many of them would reject His warnings. He tried in vain for 40 years to turn the nation of Israel back to their God.

Even though Isaiah might have been unsuccessful in bringing about his people's repentance, he recorded some of the most famous and most beautiful prophecies in the Bible. In fact, Jesus began His ministry by reading one of the prophecies written by Isaiah, a prophecy about the coming Messiah: "The Spirit of the LORD *is* upon Me, because He has anointed Me to preach the gospel to *the* poor; He has sent Me to heal the brokenhearted, to proclaim liberty to *the* captives and recovery of sight to *the* blind, to set at liberty those who are oppressed; to proclaim the acceptable year of the LORD" (Luke 4:18, 19).

Island of Misfit Toys

From the animated *Rudolph the Red-Nosed Reindeer, a*n island where unwanted and defective toys make their home (*see* Rudolph the Red-Nosed Reindeer).

It's a Wonderful Life

Based on a story by Philip Van Doren Stern, *The Greatest Gift,* the film is director Frank Capra's enduring holiday classic. Filmed in 1946 and released January 7, 1947, *It's a Wonderful Life* featured James Stewart, Donna Reed, Lionel Barrymore, Thomas Mitchell, and Henry Travers, among others. It's the story of George Bailey, who has spent his entire life sacrificing his dreams for the sake of others, culminating in one fateful Christmas Eve, when George despairs of life. Enter Clarence, George's guardian angel, who shows George what life would have been like had George never been born and the tremendous impact George's life has had on the lives of others. *It's a Wonderful*

Life is considered by the American Film Institute to be one of the best films ever made. Philip Van Doren Stern wrote the story in the late '30s and tried unsuccessfully to sell it to magazines. In 1943, he printed his story and enclosed it in his Christmas card to family and friends. RKO Pictures purchased the rights to the story for $10,000 and intended it to be a vehicle for actor Cary Grant. RKO's plans for Cary Grant never materialized, and they ended up selling the rights to Frank Capra. This was a fortunate turn of events for us all. Cary Grant was a fine actor, but it's hard to imagine anyone other than Jimmy Stewart playing George Bailey. The movie was not an immediate success; it was lukewarm at the box office. Over the years, however, it found its way to television, where slowly but surely it developed an immense fan following. Today the movie is treasured as a timeless classic.

Ivy

A climbing vine with smooth, shiny evergreen leaves (*see* Holly and the Ivy).

Trivia

The rhyme *'Twas the Night Before Christmas* sometimes goes by another name:

a. "To All a Good Night"
b. "Visions of Sugarplums"
c. "It's the Worst Shopping Experience of the Year"
d. "A Visit from St. Nicholas"

Answer: D. It is rumored, but not proven, that Clement Clarke Moore penned the poem in 1822.

Jack Frost

Jack Frost is the personification of winter. His origins are unknown. Some attribute Jack Frost's beginning to Viking folklore; others believe he originated in a Russian fairy tale. No matter where he came from, he's well known today and has even had a movie named after him. It was released in 1998 and starred Michael Keaton and Kelly Preston.

Jelly, Bowl of

See Bowl Full of Jelly.

Jerusalem

Jerusalem was the capital city of Israel from the time of David in the Old Testament until after the close of the New Testament. Jerusalem is God's Holy City, the place of many of the major events in both the Old and New Testaments and the subject of many biblical prophecies. When the

wise men came searching for the King of the Jews, the Messiah, they naturally began their search in Jerusalem. It was in the temple at Jerusalem that a 12-year-old Jesus amazed the religious leaders with His knowledge of the Scriptures. It was also from here that the adult Jesus drove out the moneychangers who were taking advantage of the worshipers visiting from surrounding cities and towns. At the end of His earthly ministry, Jesus was eventually crucified, buried, and resurrected just outside the Holy City of Jerusalem.

Jesse Tree

The family tree of Jesus Christ. Also known as the Tree of Jesse, which refers to a passage in the Book of Isaiah describing the ascent of the Messiah (Isaiah 11:1–3). The Tree of Jesse was a popular theme for medieval artists.

Jesus Christ

Jesus is undeniably the most important Person in human history. His brief life and teachings have had more impact on the world than any single life before or since. Jesus was born in Bethlehem, a town just south of Jerusalem, but He was raised in the town of Nazareth in Galilee. This is why He is sometimes referred to as "Jesus of Nazareth." He is also known as "Jesus Christ," meaning "Jesus, the Anointed One," because He is the Messiah, or "Christ," who was prophesied over hundreds of years by various prophets whose words are recorded in the

Old Testament. The Messiah was to be the Son of God, the Savior of God's people, and ultimately, the Savior of the entire world.

What is interesting is that so many people believe that Jesus is the Messiah, in spite of the fact that He was born under very lowly circumstances into what seemed like a very unexceptional family. He was born to a woman named Mary and her husband, Joseph, a carpenter; and His time in the spotlight was actually very brief. Yet the things Jesus was reported to have said and done during this brief time of ministry are truly miraculous; and the fact that those who were closest to Him were willing to die violently, rather than give up their claim that He was the Son of God, speaks volumes. Many of Jesus' teachings have gone on to become the most famous words in recorded history; and the record of His life, as found in the Bible, is the best-selling book of all time.

Many who lived before Jesus and who believed in the coming of the Messiah spent much of their time studying the prophecies surrounding His birth, life, and death. Countless millions who have lived since the time of Jesus who believe He was the Messiah have spent much of their time studying these same prophecies, along with the actual New Testament accounts of His birth, life, and death. Millions of Christians the world over call Jesus their Lord and Savior today. Although no one knows the exact date of His birth, December 25 (Christmas Day) has been set aside to celebrate the birth of Jesus Christ, the Son of God, into the world.

Jingle Bells

One of the most popular and best-known Christmas carols, "Jingle Bells" was composed by James Lord Pierpont (1822–1893) in the 1850s. It has been recorded by hundreds of artists and was the first song broadcast from space in 1965 by astronauts Wally Schirra and Tom Stafford, who were riding in a vehicle a lot more advanced than a one-horse open sleigh.

John the Baptist

The Old Testament mentions heralds, officers who ran ahead of a king to announce his coming or make his proclamations known to the people. John the Baptist is considered the herald or forerunner of Jesus because his ministry prepared people for the arrival of the Jesus who was truly the King of kings. John did this by calling people to repent and be baptized for their sins and by telling them about the One who would come after him. Even though Jesus was a relative of John the Baptist, John did not know that Jesus was the Messiah until Jesus came to John to be baptized. At that moment, God revealed to John that Jesus was His Son, the Messiah.

John was a faithful forerunner who humbly stepped aside when Jesus stepped onto the scene. John sent his own disciples to follow Jesus and willingly watched his own ministry diminish as Jesus' following grew. Due to John's uncompromising character and bold preaching, he was eventually imprisoned and beheaded by Herod. Because of the New Covenant, which started with Jesus, even those who are "least in the kingdom of heaven" are considered "greater" than John because of a superior Covenant. However, Jesus did consider John, the last of the Old Testament prophets, the greatest of them all.

Joseph

"Joseph" was the name of several men in the Old and New Testaments. "Joseph" was the name of Jesus' earthly father, husband to Jesus' mother, Mary. Not very much is known about Joseph; in fact, none of his words were even recorded in the Gospels. Although he is mentioned up until Jesus' appearance in the temple at the age of 12, he is never mentioned after Jesus begins His adult ministry. For this reason, many Bible scholars believe that Joseph died prior to Jesus' ministry. But the Scriptures do tell us

that Joseph was a carpenter and a "righteous man." And we see at least a little glimpse of his character and his faith in the considerate way that he treated Mary and in the humble way that he followed God.

Joy An emotion of great happiness, intense delight (*see* Comfort and Joy).

Joy to the World A Christmas carol with Isaac Watts's words based on scripture, and Lowell Mason's music, which is believed to have been adapted from an older melody by Handel.

Trivia

Which U.S. president first "pushed the button"—and lighted the National Christmas Tree?

a. Grover Cleveland
b. Teddy Roosevelt
c. Calvin Coolidge
d. Franklin D. Roosevelt

Answer: C. Coolidge lit the National Christmas Tree on December 24, 1923.

Jubilee

A year-long celebration that takes place the 50th year (after seven cycles of seven years) in the Hebrew religion. The Year of Jubilee was a year of celebration; there was no sowing or reaping during this year (Leviticus 25:23). The Year of Jubilee represented freedom; it gave people a chance to start over. Persons who had incurred debts and who had sold themselves as slaves or servants to others were set at liberty. It was a time of great rejoicing. Jubilee was a foreshadowing of the ministry of Jesus, who came to set people free from the slavery of sin once and for all.

Judea

Judea was another name for the land of Judah in the nation of Israel. It was bordered by the Mediterranean Sea on the west, the Dead Sea on the east, and its boundaries measured about 56 miles from east to west and north to south. The land of Judea includes the Holy City of Jerusalem, as well as the Old Testament city of Jericho.

Kin A person's family, relatives; a group of persons descended from a common ancestor; of the same nature.

King A monarch; ruler of a kingdom or territory; a male sovereign.

King of Israel God Himself was Israel's king, but the people insisted on an earthly king. The prophet Samuel anointed Saul as the first king of the Hebrew nation; however, God viewed Israel's insistence on having a king as an act of rebellion (1 Samuel 8). Saul was followed by David as king; David was succeeded by his son Solomon, one of the richest kings the world has ever seen and known for his great wisdom (*see* David, King).

Kringle, Kris

See Claus, Santa.

Kris Kringle

See Claus, Santa.

Kwanzaa

A harvest festival celebrated by some African-American communities from December 26 to January 1st. Founded during the 1960s, Kwanzaa is a celebration of the traditional African values of, among other things, family, community, and self-improvement, as well as African culture.

Trivia

You're celebrating Christmas in Africa. Which of the following are you *not* likely to see?

a. Fireworks
b. Mistletoe
c. Fruitcake
d. Caroling

Answer: B. Mistletoe tends to grow in Europe and North America.

Lamb of God

The New Testament portion of the Bible often refers to Jesus as a lamb. John the Baptist even called Him "the Lamb of God who takes away the sin of the world!" (John 1:29). This is a direct reference to the sacrifice of lambs under the Old Covenant. In order for the sins of the people to be forgiven, a perfect lamb without spot or blemish was sacrificed. Its blood was spilled to cover the sins of the people for one year. This sacrifice of animals was a foreshadowing of the sacrifice of Jesus on the cross. His blood was spilled to cover the sins of all humankind. However, unlike animal sacrifices that had to be repeated, Jesus' sacrifice removes all sin once and for all because He was a truly blameless sacrifice, which was once signified by a "spotless lamb."

Leg Lamp

From the movie *A Christmas Story*, the leg lamp was Old Man Parker's major award. The movie has gained such a following that a replica of the leg lamp featured in the film is available for purchase. Now you can give your loved ones their own "major award" this Christmas (*see* A Christmas Story).

Letters to Santa

Many children write impassioned letters to Santa Claus, listing what they hope to receive from him for Christmas. Surprisingly, many of these letters to Santa actually wind up at North Pole, Alaska. Local residents there volunteer as "Santa's helpers," answering all the letters that have return addresses. In 2005, Santa's helpers answered over 120,000 letters to Santa.

Lighting of the Christmas Tree in Washington

Since 1923, the United States has had a tradition of lighting a National Christmas Tree in Washington, D.C. Well-known entertainers perform, and the president brings a message of hope and peace to the world. In addition, the lighting of a second Christmas tree located at the Capitol Building in Washington, D.C., has been a tradition since 1964.

Lights

At Christmastime, festive lights decorate indoor and outdoor trees, homes, and buildings. A few centuries ago, Christmas trees were lit by candles that were attached to the branches with melted wax or pins. Later, small lanterns held the candles. During this period, many families did not put up their Christmas tree until December 24, due to danger of fire. Electric lights for Christmas trees came into existence in 1882 when Edward Johnson, an associate of Thomas Edison, hand-wired colored bulbs and strung them around an evergreen tree. Albert Sadacca, who came up with the idea of painting the bulbs in various colors, is credited with popularizing Christmas tree lights. Albert and his brothers started the NOMA Electric Company, which remained the largest Christmas lighting company in the world until 1965. Today, NOMA bulbs are sought after by collectors and can still be found through online auctions.

Linen

Linen is a fabric woven from flax or hemp fibers. In biblical times, garments made of linen helped keep the wearer cool in hot weather. Because fine linen was expensive, it was worn by kings, queens, and other members of royalty. Many of the depictions of pharaohs and other royals found in Egyptian tombs show the royals dressed in linen garments. After the death of Jesus, His body was wrapped in white linen (Luke 23:53; John 19:40).

Linus

Linus is a character from the Charles Schulz comic strip *Peanuts* and a friend to Charlie Brown. As Charlie Brown tries in vain to discover what Christmas is really all about, Linus helps him out by reciting Luke 2:8–14 from the King James Version of the Bible: "And there were in the same country shepherds abiding in the field, keeping watch over their flock by night. And, lo, the angel of the Lord came upon them, and the glory of the Lord shone round about them: and they were sore afraid. And the angel said unto them, Fear not: for, behold, I bring you good tidings of great joy, which shall be to all people. For unto you is born this day in the city of David a Saviour, which is Christ the Lord. And this *shall be* a sign unto you; Ye shall find the babe wrapped in swaddling clothes lying in a manger. And suddenly there was with the angel a multitude of the heavenly host praising God, and saying, Glory to God in the highest, and on earth peace, good will toward men." (*See* Charlie Brown.)

Lion

A large, tawny-colored cat, native to Africa and southern Asia, and often called the "King of the Jungle." The lion is the traditional symbol for the Hebrew tribe of Judah. In Christian tradition, the Lion of Judah is believed to represent Jesus.

List

A written series of names or items, such as Santa's list of little girls and boys, showing who has been naughty and who has been nice.

Little Drummer Boy

See Drummer Boy.

Little Match Girl

A Danish fairy tale by Hans Christian Anderson, published in 1848, which tells the tragic story of a poor little girl who sold matches on the city streets and froze to death on New Year's Eve.

Live Nativity

See Drive-Thru Nativity.

Lord

God actually has a proper name, which He revealed to His people in the Old Testament. This name was considered too holy to be spoken aloud by the Israelites. Therefore, whenever an Israelite read aloud a passage of Scripture that included the proper name of God, he was expected to substitute another name. One such substitution was *Adonai,* which means "my Lord."

The name of God appears as *YHWH* in the ancient Old Testament writings. This is known as the Tetragrammaton. As translators labored to render the Old Testament writings faithfully into English, they had to decide how most accurately to translate the Tetragrammaton. Many chose to render the name simply as "LORD" in keeping with the original Jewish tradition and because it was impossible to distinguish the proper spelling and pronunciation of God's proper name anyway.

Lord's Day

Sunday is considered the first day of the week and is also called "the Lord's Day" because many believe that Sunday was the day Jesus rose from the dead. Sunday is often mistakenly considered the Sabbath, which was the Jewish day of rest. However, the Sabbath is actually the last day of the week, or Saturday. No matter the day of the week, most Christians still set aside at least one particular day of the week to worship together with other Christians.

Love

A deep feeling of personal attachment for another person. The Bible tells us that God is love. It does not say that He *has* love, but that He *is* love itself. The best definition of love can be found in 1 Corinthians 13.

Lowing

The mooing of cattle. Most are familiar with this term because it is what woke the poor babe in the popular Christmas carol "Away in a Manger."

Luke

Luke was the author of the Gospel of Luke and the Book of Acts. He was a physician and a "fellow laborer" with the apostle Paul, accompanying him on at least a few of his missionary journeys. Luke was also the only non-

Jewish author of any of the New Testament writings. His Gospel shows his concern for the sick and the poor. Perhaps Luke's great compassion for the helpless is why Paul referred to him as "the beloved physician" and why his retelling of Jesus' birth story was so tender. You can find this account in Luke 2.

Lump of Coal

What naughty little boys and girls have traditionally found in their stockings, instead of candy or desirable gifts.

Trivia

In one famous episode of *The Simpsons,* Homer loses his Christmas money at the dog track, but brings home a new family pet, a dim-witted greyhound named:

a. Santa's Little Helper
b. Saint Nick
c. Blitzen
d. Candy Cane

Answer: A. When Santa's Little Helper loses his race, his owner abandons him. Homer takes the dog home as a Christmas gift.

M

Macy's

A chain of department stores, founded in 1858 by Rowland H. Macy in New York City. Sponsor of the Macy's Thanksgiving Day Parade since the 1920s. (*See* Miracle on 34th Street.)

Macy's Thanksgiving Day Parade

The biggest and best of the Thanksgiving Day parades, sponsored by Macy's Department Store since 1924. The parade is known for its gigantic helium-filled balloons, and the final float in the parade belongs to Santa himself (*see* Macy's).

Magi

This is another name for the wise men from the East, who followed a star to locate the infant Jesus and honored Him by bringing gifts of gold, frankincense, and myrrh. Tradition holds that there were three magi, but that assumption is based on the mention of three gifts. The names of the magi are unknown, but tradition has named them Caspar, Balthasar, and Melchior.

Magnificat of Mary

This is also called the Canticle of Mary or Song of Mary and can be found in Luke 1:46–55. The Magnificat is Mary's prayer of praise in response to her cousin Elizabeth's greeting.

Maids

Female servants. In the song "The Twelve Days of Christmas," there are eight maids a' milking. (*See* Twelve Days of Christmas.)

Malachi

Not much is known about the Old Testament prophet Malachi. He prophesied during the time when Nehemiah led the Israelites in rebuilding the wall of Jerusalem after their captivity. Malachi is known for his strong words condemning the Israelites' negligence in paying 10 percent of their income to the temple. This 10 percent is known as a tithe, and it was the only means of financial support for the Old Testament temple and the priesthood.

Malachi is also known for his prophecy about the return of Elijah, who would go ahead of the Lord to prepare God's people for the coming of the Messiah. Before John the Baptist's birth, the angel Gabriel appeared to his father,

Zacharias, and referenced Malachi's prophecy. He used it to tell Zacharias that John would act in "the spirit and power of Elijah." John did, in fact, become a type of Elijah in that he prepared God's people for the coming of Jesus Christ. He even adopted Elijah's signature camel-hair clothes and leather belt.

Mall

A large complex consisting of several stores and sometimes other businesses, such as restaurants and theatres. It's a great place not to be on Christmas Eve!

Manger

A trough or box from which animals eat, usually found inside a stable or barn. The baby Jesus lay in a manger (Luke 2:12, 16).

Mantle

A cloak or cape; also, something that covers. This term is heard often during the Christmas season in the beginning strains of "Winter Wonderland."

March of the Wooden Soldiers

See Babes in Toyland.

Marley

Ebenezer Scrooge's dead friend, Jacob Marley, whose chain-laden ghost visits Scrooge to warn him of what is about to take place on one haunting Christmas Eve (*see* A Christmas Carol).

Marshmallows

Spongy, sweet, edible confections consisting of sugar, corn syrup, and gelatin, among other things, and usually white in color. These are suitable for toasting over campfires (preferably at the end of a stick) or stringing into confectionary garlands for the decorating of trees and homes.

Mary

The mother of Jesus, a descendant of the line of David. It was common in Mary's time for Jewish women to become betrothed as very young girls. Mary had only just become betrothed to Joseph at the time of Jesus' conception, so she may have been as young as 13 years old.

Melchior

See Magi.

Melchizedek

Abraham went to war with Chedorlaomer and his allies in order to rescue his nephew Lot. Upon defeating Chedorlaomer and the other kings, Melchizedek, king of Salem and priest of God Most High, brought out bread and wine for Abraham. He blessed Abraham, and Abraham gave him one-tenth of all the spoils from his victory. Because this is the only encounter with Melchizedek in the Old Testament, he is something of a mysterious figure. He is also seen as a foreshadowing of Christ, who would later become our true High Priest and offer His own flesh and blood as a sacrifice to pay for our sins. We remember Jesus and His sacrifice when we eat the bread and drink the fruit of the vine during Communion (*see* Eucharist).

Memories

The recollection of past events and experiences. Some of the most precious and special memories are often of Christmases past.

Menorah

The menorah used in the celebration of Hanukkah is a nine-branched candelabrum, which is lit during the eight days of Hanukkah (*see* Hanukkah).

Merry

Festively joyous, as in *Merry Christmas.*

Merry Christmas

A greeting during the season in which Christ's (Jesus') birth is celebrated. The literal meaning would be something like: "May you be filled with joy and cheer as you remember the birth of Christ and all that means to you."

Merry Gentlemen

From "God Rest Ye Merry Gentlemen," one of the oldest known Christmas carols, reputedly dating back to the 15th century.

Messiah

See Christ.

Trivia

A choreographer named Marius Petipa commissioned Tchaikovsky to write music for *The Nutcracker* ballet when?

a. 1956.
b. 1912.
c. 1891.
d. 1885.

Micah There are a number of Micahs mentioned in the Bible. One of them, the author of the Book of Micah, was a young contemporary of the prophet Isaiah. Micah prophesied that Bethlehem would be the place of the Messiah's birth (5:2).

Michael An archangel referred to in Scripture as a great prince who stands for (fights for, is a guardian to) God's people (Daniel 10:21; 12:1). When Satan rebels against God, Michael and his angels fight against him (Revelation 12:7).

Answer: Tchaikovsky's music helped transform *The Nutcracker and the Mouse*, a book by E. T. A. Hoffman, into a much-loved ballet in 1891.

Midnight Mass

A midnight mass (worship service) is celebrated by many Catholics on Christmas Eve. These can be quite beautiful and moving.

Midwife

A person, generally female, experienced in assisting women in childbirth. Midwives have been around since ancient times and can still be found today. While most women will opt for a hospital and obstetrician, some prefer natural childbirth with the assistance of a midwife. Scripture doesn't indicate whether Mary had anyone to assist her with the birth of Jesus, and she certainly didn't enjoy the relative comforts of an inn with bed and heat. Instead, she gave birth in a cave that served as a shelter for animals.

Mincemeat

A pie filling that in earlier times was comprised of spiced meat and fruit. The more modern version of the mince pie contains dried fruit, spices, and nuts and is a traditional British pastry, usually made during the Christmas holiday.

Miracle on 34th Street

From 1947, one of the all-time great Christmas movies, starring Maureen O'Hara, John Payne, Natalie Wood, and Edmund Gwenn. When Macy's Department Store hires a department store Santa to appear in their Thanksgiving Day Parade, he turns out to be the real thing. But the single mother and her daughter (O'Hara and Wood) both take some convincing. Mr. Kringle (Gwenn) is accused of being mentally incompetent and is taken to court, where his sanity is defended by attorney John Payne. The court's decision declares Mr. Kringle to be Santa, and Wood and O'Hara both become believers (*see* Macy's Thanksgiving Day Parade).

Misfit Toys

Unwanted and defective toys who make their home on the Island of Misfit Toys in the animated film *Rudolph the Red-Nosed Reindeer* (*see* Island of Misfit Toys; *see also* Rudolph the Red-Nosed Reindeer).

Mistletoe

A plant that grows as a parasite on various trees and that is traditionally used in Christmas decorations. The European mistletoe, native to Great Britain and much of Europe, has smooth-edged oval leaves in pairs along a woody stem and has clusters of white berries of six or less. The American version has broader, shorter leaves and clusters of 10 or more berries. If you're caught standing under a bunch of mistletoe with another person, you are expected to share a kiss—a tradition, which may have its roots in ancient fertility rites.

Moore, Clement C.

Clement C. Moore (1779–1863) was a professor of Greek and Oriental literature, but is best known as the American author of *'Twas the Night Before Christmas*. However, his authorship has been questioned by some who believe the celebrated poem may have been written by Henry Livingston, Jr. Mr. Livingston's descendants have fought a long-running battle to have his authorship recognized. A case is made against Moore's authorship in Professor Donald Foster's book *Author Unknown: On the Trail of Anonymous*. (*See* 'Twas the Night Before Christmas.)

Mortal

Subject to death; the weak and fleeting nature of human life.

Although Jesus is the third Person of the Trinity and fully divine, He allowed Himself to be clothed in flesh to become fully man. He was born of a virgin and experienced mortal life and mortal, physical death—all this because of His great love for each of us.

Mouse

The creature who was not stirring in *'Twas the Night Before Christmas*. However, his fierce cousin, the Mouse King, is very busy appearing in *The Nutcracker Ballet*, based on the story *The Nutcracker and the King of Mice*.

Mrs. Claus

The spouse of Santa Claus (*see* Claus, Santa).

Mulled Wine

A traditional winter drink made from wine (usually red), which contains spices and is served hot. Apparently, a former holiday favorite of Clarence the Angel, at least when served "heavy on the cinnamon and light on the cloves" (*see* It's a Wonderful Life).

Myra

There are so many legends surrounding the historical Saint Nicholas that it is very difficult to separate fact from fiction. Stories abound about this man and his legendary generosity. However, one fact that is generally held to be true is that he was a bishop in Myra, which is now part of modern-day Turkey (*see* Saint Nicholas).

Myrrh

An aromatic gum resin from a small spiny tree, used to make incense and perfume. Myrrh figured in Jesus' life at the beginning of His life and at the end of His life. It was a gift brought by the wise men when He was born; according to Mark 15:23, it was also in a drink (wine mingled with myrrh) that was given to Him as He hung, dying upon the cross (*see* Magi).

Mystery Anything that is kept secret or that remains unexplained. In the New Testament, *mystery* refers to a secret that God reveals to His servants through His Holy Spirit, and Jesus refers to the kingdom of God as a mystery (Matthew 13:11; Mark 4:11; Luke 8:10).

Trivia

What is traditional wassailing?

a. A Swedish practice similar to yodeling.
b. Going door to door, singing for refreshments.
c. Going door-to-door to hand out cards bearing the image of a saint.
d. The snoring noise made by Aunt Bertha after turkey dinner.

Answer: B. In Europe, carolers were often rewarded with a drink called wassail.

Name Tags Small tags made of paper or cardboard, which are fastened to Christmas gifts and bear the name of the recipient and the giver.

Natal Star Jesus' birth star, the Star of Bethlehem.

National Lampoon's Christmas Vacation A 1989 film, the third film in the *National Lampoon's Vacation* series, featuring the intrepid Griswold family (Chevy Chase as Clark Griswold, Beverly D'Angelo as

Ellen Griswold, and Juliette Lewis and Johnny Galecki as the Griswold siblings; Randy Quaid and Miriam Flynn as Cousin Eddie and Cousin Catherine). When Clark's employer sends him a gift of jelly instead of his anticipated hefty Christmas bonus, the frustration and disappointment are too much for Clark. Cousin Eddie decides to intervene by kidnapping Clark's boss. The movie is entertaining, and it's great fun to join the Griswolds and the Clarks in their shenanigans each Christmas season.

Nativity The birth of Jesus Christ.

Naughty Mischievous, disobedient. What you don't want to be if you hope to receive presents from Santa.

Nazareth A town in northern Israel; the childhood home of Jesus Christ. Because of His close association with Nazareth, Jesus became known as Jesus of Nazareth.

Nice The opposite of naughty; what you have to be in order for your name to be on Santa's list of good little boys and girls (*see* Naughty).

Night

The hours of darkness; the period between sunset and sunrise. Santa Claus makes his annual delivery of Christmas gifts at night.

Noel

A Christmas carol; also, the French name given to the Christmas season; Yuletide.

North Pole

The northernmost point of Earth; the traditional home of Santa Claus (*see* Claus, Santa).

Nutcracker

A device used for cracking the shells of nuts. Also, a ballet which is immensely popular at Christmastime, *The Nutcracker*, based on the 1800s story *The Nutcracker and the Mouse King* by the German writer E. T. A. Hoffmann. It tells the story of Clara, a young girl who is given a nutcracker as a Christmas gift. Clara falls asleep with the nutcracker in her arms and has a magical dream in which her nutcracker must battle the fierce Mouse King. Eventually, the nutcracker turns into a prince and takes Clara to visit the Land of Snow and the Land of Sweets. A sugar plum fairy and cavalier are also featured in the ballet.

Trivia

All of these people died Christmas Day, except:

a. James Brown
b. Dean Martin
c. Charlie Chaplin
d. Hank Williams

Answer: D. Hank Williams passed away New Year's Day, 1953.

O

Oliver Cromwell *See* Cromwell, Oliver.

Omnipotence Having unlimited power or authority; one of the attributes of God.

Omnipresence One who is present everywhere at the same time; one of the attributes of God.

Omniscience Possessing infinite knowledge; one of the attributes of God.

Operation Christmas Child

A project that began in the United Kingdom in 1990 and that was adopted by Samaritan's Purse (1993), a Christian missionary organization, which focuses on aid to children, particularly in countries torn by war or by disaster. Operation Christmas Child enlists thousands of volunteer gift-givers to supply gifts to needy children every year.

Orange

An edible citrus fruit, which makes its way into stockings at Christmas. In days gone by, oranges and other types of fruit were the most common gifts found in stockings on Christmas morning.

Ornaments

Embellishments or adornments. At Christmastime, we decorate Christmas trees by hanging ornaments from the branches and use them to otherwise "deck the halls" and to give packages pizzazz. Ornaments can range from children's construction paper bells to handblown, pricey collectibles. High sentimental value is often attached to them, no matter what they cost in dollars and cents.

Outdoor Lights

Christmas lights that are strung outdoors. They can be found hanging from rooftops, house fronts, shrubbery, trees, and mailboxes. They may be used to form reindeer and Santa, angels and presents, snow people and nativities, and a multitude of other light-bedecked sculptures (some actually animated). In contests throughout the country, prizes are awarded to the homes that boast the largest number of single lights. The resulting glow from these homes can bc seen for miles as hundreds of thousands of little bulbs light the night skies and send electric bills soaring (*see* Lights).

Over the River and Through the Woods

The very vague directions given to grandmother's house in the Christmas carol by the same name.

Trivia

Artists have produced many hilarious Christmas song parodies and spoofs. Which of the following is not an actual song?

a. "I Ran Over a Headlit Deer"
b. "The Night Santa Went Crazy"
c. "Five Months of Bills"
d. "Wreck the Malls"

Answer: A. "The Night Santa Went Crazy" is by Weird Al Yankovic; Bob Rivers is responsible for the other two songs.

P

Packages Tied Up with String

See Favorite Things.

Palestine

The biblical name for Palestine is Canaan, also known as the Holy Land or the Land of Israel. Palestine is located between the Jordan River and the Mediterranean Sea. God promised this land to Abraham and his descendants (*see* Covenant). Judaism, Christianity, and Islam all have their roots in Palestine. It is the land of Jesus' birth.

Papyrus

A writing material prepared from strips of the papyrus plant and used by the ancient Egyptians, Romans, and Greeks. The ark in which baby Moses was hidden by his family is believed to have been made of papyrus plants. The majority of the Dead Sea Scrolls, as well as the oldest manuscripts of the New Testament (including the Christmas story), were written on papyrus.

Passion Play

From medieval times to present day, a dramatic presentation of the trial, suffering, and death of Jesus Christ, the Son of God. Jesus was born into our world to die for our sins and to offer us the promise of eternal life.

Past, Ghost of Christmas

See A Christmas Carol.

Pax Romana

The peace enforced by ancient Rome on the dominions of its empire. Caesar Augustus is credited with leading Rome into a long period of enforced peace (*see* Augustus, Caesar) and was the emperor when Jesus was born.

Peace

A state of harmony; not at war. The Bible speaks of peace that passes understanding. With the peace that God brings through the work of His Son Jesus Christ, there can be chaos around you, but quiet within your soul.

Peace on Earth

God's desire for us, which probably will not be fully realized until Christ returns. When the angels proclaimed Jesus' birth to the shepherds, they praised God with the words "Glory to God in the highest, and on earth peace, goodwill toward men!" (Luke 2:14).

Peal

A loud, lengthy ringing of bells.

Piñata

A gaily decorated papier-mâché figure or container filled with goodies like toys and candy and suspended in the air. Blindfolded children take turns swinging a stick, hoping to knock down the piñata and release its contents.

Associated with Hispanic culture, the piñata may have originated in China. The piñata once held religious symbolism; but today, most connect its use with fun celebrations. Piñatas are especially popular in Hispanic culture during traditional Christmas processions, which help to usher in the Christmas season.

Pine

An evergreen, coniferous tree (*see* Christmas Tree).

Pinecones

The cones of a pine tree (*see* Pine).

Plum Pudding

Also known as Christmas Pudding, this is the traditional end to the British holiday dinner. Christmas Pudding dates as far back as the 14th century, but it was very different from the Plum Pudding of today. The earliest Christmas or Plum Pudding was more like a soup or porridge and was made with mutton and beef, assorted fruits, and spices. Toward the end of the 1500s, it started to resemble Plum Pudding as we know it, with the addition of breadcrumbs, eggs, and spirits; by the 1600s, it had become a traditional Christmas Pudding. However, the Puritans banned it as being too rich for godly people. Eventually, it was reinstated; and by Victorian times, it once again became part of traditional holiday fare. An old custom called for putting a silver coin into the Plum Pudding; it was supposed to bring good luck to whoever found it. Today, you don't have to live in the United Kingdom to enjoy Plum Pudding. If you can't find one where you live, you can order one online.

Poinsettia

Native to Central America, the poinsettia plant flourished in Mexico and was used by the ancient Aztecs to make textiles, cosmetics, and medicine to treat fever. The poinsettia gets its name from Joel Roberts Poinsett (1779–1851), the first U.S. ambassador to Mexico. Poinsett (who later founded the Smithsonian Institution) was an avid lover of botany. He had his own greenhouse in South Carolina; after discovering the beautiful plant with the vibrant red leaves, he sent some back to South Carolina and began cultivating them.

The legend of the poinsettia tells of Pepita, a poor Mexican girl who had no gift to bring to the Christ Child at Christmas Eve services. Her cousin Pedro encouraged her, telling her that even the most humble gift, if given in love, is acceptable in the eyes of the Lord. So Pepita knelt by the roadside and picked some weeds to make a bouquet, the best gift she was able to bring. When she brought her gift and placed it at the foot of the nativity scene, her little weeds burst into brilliant red blooms. Everyone who saw it believed they had witnessed a Christmas miracle. The plant came to be called the *Flores de Nocha Buena,* or Flowers of the Holy Night, because they bloomed each year during the Christmas season. Today, it is an enduring symbol of Christmas.

Polar Pertaining to the North Pole or South Pole.

Polar Express, The An animated film from 2004, *The Polar Express* was based on the book by Chris Van Allsburg (recipient of the Caldecott Medal), first published in 1985. The film featured the voice of Tom Hanks not only as the conductor, but in several other parts. On Christmas Eve, a young boy full of doubts about Santa Claus boards a magical train bound for the North Pole with many other children. The film was directed by Robert Zemeckis, who also wrote the screenplay.

Polish Foods

During the Christmas holiday, diners can enjoy many traditional Polish dishes that are rarely prepared at any other time. Traditionally, 12 dishes are served on Christmas Eve. The dishes vary from region to region and sometimes from family to family. Some typical dishes might include a piernik (honey cake), babka z rumen (rum baba), or cwibak (Christmas fruitcake).

Pontius Pilate

During Jesus' time, governor of the Roman province of Judea. When the infant Jesus was born in a stable, His birth changed the destiny of several historical figures, including that of Pontius Pilate. According to Scripture, Pontius Pilate presided over the trial of Jesus and reluctantly ordered His crucifixion. The birth and death of Jesus would change not only Pontius Pilate's destiny, but the destinies of all humankind.

Popcorn

When the first European settlers came to America, how surprised they must have been when they were introduced to popcorn by the Native Americans! Popcorn is made from kernels of corn, which puff up or "pop" when heated. It used to be strung as garland for decorating Christmas trees and sometimes still is by those who want to recreate an old-fashioned Christmas!

Postmark

An official mark stamped on letters or other mail and indicating where and when something was mailed. At Christmastime, many children love receiving letters or packages postmarked North Pole (*see* Letters to Santa).

Praise

An act of worship; to honor with a song or with words and/or the raising of hands. The Bible calls praise a sacrifice, one of the few sacrifices that are acceptable, even pleasing, to God. Angels raised their voices in praise as they announced Jesus' birth.

Prancer

One of Santa's reindeer (*see* Blitzen).

Prayer

Conversation with God. The Bible tells us to pray without ceasing, not just when we get in a jam and need God to bail us out. It's about relationship, setting aside time to spend with God and Him alone. God listens to our prayers and cares about the longing of our hearts. Examples of this in Scripture would be the prayers of Simeon and Anna. Both had a personal relationship with God; both prayed to see the Messiah, and God heard and answered their prayers (Luke 2:25–38).

Preexistent Deity

To talk about the Preexistent Deity of Christ is to recognize that He was part of the Trinity before He took on His human existence through the Incarnation. This is an important point because it helps us appreciate what Jesus sacrificed in order to become Immanuel, "God with Us." It shows Christ's humility and sets an example for us as well: "Let this mind be in you which was also in Christ Jesus, who, being in the form of God, did not consider it robbery to be equal with God, but made Himself of no reputation, taking the form of a bondservant, *and* coming in the likeness of men" (Philippians 2:5–7).

Prelit

See Fiber Optic Lights.

Present, Ghost of Christmas

See A Christmas Carol.

Presents

Gifts. At Christmastime, Christians give presents to celebrate the great gift God gave by sending His Son, Jesus, to be born into our world.

Prophecy

A prediction of what is to come. Prophecy is not reading a horoscope or tuning in to the latest psychic or feel-good guru. Prophecy from God is a divinely inspired instruction, prediction, or exhortation given through a prophet of God (*see* Prophet). The prophets of God were often called to deliver messages the recipients did not want to hear. They were sometimes also called to do things that people did not understand, but that held great spiritual significance (such as Hosea's being called to marry an unfaithful wife). Many Old Testament prophecies looked forward to the Messiah's (Jesus') birth, ministry, death, and resurrection.

Prophet

In the Bible, a prophet was a messenger from God, a human being called to deliver a divine message. For example, several of the Old Testament prophets proclaimed Jesus' birth years before it took place. The test of a prophet was whether or not his prophecies came to pass. His life was on the line; he could be stoned if his prophecies did not come true. Nevertheless, there were false prophets then, just as there are false prophets now. How do you tell the difference? By prayer, by checking everything against Scripture (God will not prophesy something that contradicts His Word), and by the leading of the Holy Spirit.

Propitiation

An appeasement; a conciliation. Jesus' birth signaled God's willingness to accept an appeasement for our sins, the only acceptable sacrifice—the spotless Lamb of God.

Providence

The care and guidance of God; His loving involvement with all of His creation. God showed His love for us most intimately by sending His Son Jesus to be born into our world. Jesus came to give us a living picture of what God is like.

Punch

A beverage consisting of fruit juices and water, sometimes with wine or other spirits added, and served in a punch bowl. Punches are popular drinks at Christmas festivities.

Quirinius A Roman aristocrat who, according to the Gospel of Luke, was governor of Syria at the time of Jesus' birth and connected with the taking of the census for tax purposes (Luke 2:1–5). Historians disagree that Quirinius was governor at the time of the census; he may have been involved in a civil capacity.

Trivia

Who tells Charlie Brown the story of Jesus' birth in *A Charlie Brown Christmas*?

a. Lucy
b. Linus
c. Sally
d. An unseen adult

Answer: B. Linus quotes the Christmas story from the Gospel of Luke.

Reign Sovereignty; royal rule or authority; the period during which a sovereign rules. While Jesus was born in less than desirable circumstances to a working class couple in a small province, He was nonetheless Majesty, born to rule and to reign.

Raiment Clothing or apparel; a garment. The first raiment worn by the Lord when He was born in a manger was what all newborns wore in His day, swaddling bands (*see* Swaddling Bands).

Ransom To redeem someone who is a prisoner or slave (*see* Redeem). Christ is known as our "Redeemer" because His birth signified the purchase of our freedom and the chance for us to have eternal life, if we choose to repent and believe in Him.

Recipe

A set of instructions, including a list of ingredients, for preparing something, particularly a food dish. Many Christmas recipes are family recipes, which are treasured and handed down from one generation to the next.

Red

One of the colors of Christmas and a reminder of Christ's blood, which was shed for us.

Red Ryder BB Gun

A BB gun made by Daisy Outdoor Products and introduced in 1938, forever immortalized in the film *A Christmas Story* (*see* A Christmas Story).

Red Suit

Louis Prang, a German immigrant who introduced Christmas cards to America, is credited with giving Santa his red suit on a card in the late 1800s. Prior to that time, Santa wore suits of various colors. Although Prang was not the first to come up with the idea of a Christmas card, he popularized the idea and became so identified with Christmas cards that he came to be known as the "Father of the Christmas card" (*see* Cards, Christmas).

Red Wagon

The most famous little red wagon is the Radio Flyer, which had its start in 1917 when a young Italian by the name of Antonio Pasin saved enough money to open a one-room workshop in Chicago, Illinois. A skilled craftsman like his father and grandfather before him, Pasin's business grew; and by 1923, he had several employees. They became known as the Liberty Coaster Company (after the Statue of Liberty) and created their first wagon, the Liberty Coaster. The handcrafted wooden Liberty Coaster wagon was the forerunner of the Radio Flyer. The company changed its name in the 1930s to Radio Steel Manufacturing Co. Pasin named his first steel wagon Radio Flyer, inspired by his fascination with the invention of the radio by fellow Italian Guglielmo Marconi and also by his fascination with flight. Thus, Radio Flyer was born; and Pasin's classic little red wagon continues to delight both children and adults many decades later—especially when found under the tree on Christmas morning.

Redeem

To recover; to buy back; in biblical terms, to deliver from sin and its consequences by offering a sacrifice in place of the sinner. As Christians, we are the redeemed of the Lord (*see* Ransom).

Reindeer

Large deer of the Arctic, having branched antlers. At least one of them is known to have a red nose (*see* Rudolph the Red-Nosed Reindeer).

Repentance

Sincere remorse for past conduct or sins; a determination to take a different course. The Messiah was born so that we would have the freedom to choose a different course and, by believing in Him, have eternal life.

Resurrection

The Resurrection of Jesus Christ from the dead is one of the most central doctrines of Christianity. Above all, it is what proves Jesus Christ is the Son of God and assures His followers of the hope of eternal life. It proves that Christ was more than just an inspired man, a great teacher, and a prophet. Belief in His triumph over death and the grave are nonnegotiable for those who claim to be Christians, that is, for those who claim to believe that Jesus is the Son of God and that He will one day raise us all from the dead. In fact, the apostle Paul spoke about faith in the Resurrection this way: "But if there is no resurrection of the dead, then Christ is not risen. And if Christ is not risen, then our preaching *is* empty and your faith *is* also empty" (1 Corinthians 15:13, 14).

Even though Paul became a Christian after the Resurrection, he had an unwavering faith in the fact that Christ was raised from the dead. As with the other apostles, it was part of the very foundation of his faith. In fact, he said: "But I do not want you to be ignorant, brethren, concerning those who have fallen asleep, lest you sorrow as others who have no hope. For if we believe that Jesus died and rose again, even so God will bring with Him those who sleep in Jesus" (1 Thessalonians 4:13, 14). And that is a great hope indeed.

Returns Things that are taken back to a retailer by a consumer. Returns are also the reason that gift cards are becoming more and more popular as presents for Christmas.

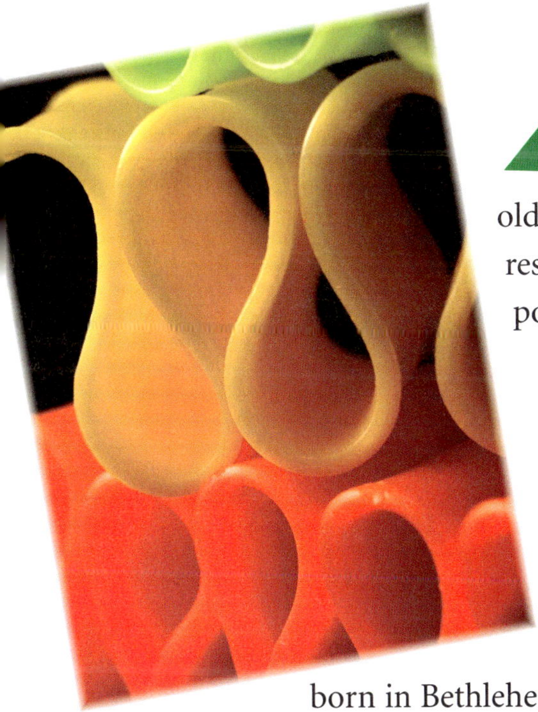

Ribbon Candy A thin, hard, old-fashioned candy made into folds that resemble ribbons, ribbon candy is especially popular at Christmastime.

Righteousness Without guilt or sin; upright; moral. For those who accept Christ, God accepts His righteousness as our own (Romans 4:3–22; Galatians 3:6; Philippians 3:9). When Christ was born in Bethlehem, heaven rejoiced because God had sent His Son, who would fulfill all righteousness and offer Himself as a sacrifice on our behalf, literally becoming our righteousness.

Trivia

In Charles Dickens's *A Christmas Carol*, the Ghost of Christmas Present opens his robes, revealing two starving children to Scrooge. Their names are:

a. Longing and Hate
b. Fear and Trembling
c. Ignorance and Want
d. Ponch and Jon

Roast Beast From *How the Grinch Stole Christmas*, the roast beast was the main course of the Christmas meal (*see* Grinch).

Roof The cover or shelter on the top of a building or dwelling. Santa tries very hard not to slide off rooftops when he lands to make his Christmas deliveries!

Answer: C. "Ignorance and Want" were twins, the sight of whom delivered a challenge to Scrooge that helping the poor is an individual responsibility.

Rudolph (The Red-nosed Reindeer)

Many of us believe that Rudolph was born in 1964 with the debut of the Rankin-Bass animated film *Rudolph the Red-Nosed Reindeer*. Others believe that Rudolph was actually born when Johnny Marks wrote and film star Gene Autry recorded a song by the same name in 1949. But Rudolph was *really* born in 1939, when Robert L. May, an employee of Montgomery Ward (department store chain), created Rudolph to be featured in a children's booklet, which his employer gave away. Since May created Rudolph as an employee and the department store held the copyright, he received no money or royalties. Under tremendous debt from medical bills due to his wife's terminal illness, May persuaded Montgomery Ward to turn the copyright over to him in 1947. His brother-in-law, songwriter Johnny Marks, turned the story into a song; and the recording by Gene Autry became a best-selling Christmas song, second only to "White Christmas."

Trivia

Match the product and its popular Christmas commercial:

a.	"We Wish You a Merry Christmas" on handbells	McDonald's
b.	Teaching the world to sing	Folgers
c.	Red-haired mascot on ice skates	Hershey's Kisses
d.	Johnny's home for Christmas	Coca-Cola

Answers: A = Hershey's; B = Coca-Cola; C = McDonald's; D = Folgers

S

Sabbath A day of rest. Among Jewish people and some Christians, this is the seventh day of the week (Saturday). Most Christians observe the first day of the week (Sunday) as their Sabbath. Now that Jesus has made a way for us to enter into God's presence, we can now enter into God's "rest" at any time (Matthew 11:28, 29).

Sacrifice Something or someone given as an offering. The sacrifices of God (those sacrifices we can give as an offering to God) are a broken heart and a contrite spirit. Praise is also an acceptable sacrifice (*see* Praise). Jesus' life was a sacrifice, an offering made on our behalf to reconcile us to God the Father.

Saint Nicholas

St. Nicholas was supposedly born during the third century in the village of Patara, which is in present-day Turkey. He was said to be a devout Christian who was made the Bishop of Myra while still a young man (*see* Myra). According to legend, he was known for his generosity and his love for children and also had a concern for ships and sailors. The traditional date of his death (December 6, A.D. 343) became a day of celebration known as St. Nicholas's Day. In Europe, the widely celebrated St. Nicholas feast day, December 6, kept alive the stories of St. Nicholas's generosity and goodness. The first Europeans to arrive in the New World brought St. Nicholas with them (Columbus named a port in Haiti for St. Nicholas on December 6, 1492). Many things contributed to the evolution of St. Nicholas to Santa Claus, including the celebrated poem *A Visit from St. Nicholas*, also known as *'Twas the Night Before Christmas* (*see* Moore, Clement C.). In 1863, a series of annual drawings by political cartoonist

Trivia

Who sang "You're a Mean One, Mr. Grinch"?

a. Thurl Ravenscroft
b. Burl Ives
c. Chuck Jones
d. Boris Karloff

Answer: A. Though Karloff is often credited for singing the famous recording, it was actually Ravenscroft, who also lent his voice to Kellogg's Frosted Flakes mascot Tony the Tiger.

Thomas Nast in *Harper's Weekly* helped establish the image of Santa Claus as a chubby man with a beard, fur garments, and a pipe. Some believe that St. Nicholas grew out of legend and was not a true historical figure. Whatever the truth may be, he lives in the hearts and minds of most people today in the form of Santa Claus (*see* Claus, Santa).

Sale

A special disposal of merchandise at a reduced price (a favorite four-letter word of any Christmas shopper).

Sales

More than one sale; even better than a sale (*see* Sale).

Salvation

Redemption; deliverance from the penalty of sin. In the Old Testament, salvation was sometimes used to describe deliverance from danger or oppression by the hand of God, such as the exodus from Egypt (Exodus 12:40—14:31). In the New Testament, a new understanding of salvation came with the ministry, death, and resurrection of Jesus Christ and our choice whether to accept and believe in Him (Acts 16:31). The whole purpose of Christ's birth was so that He might purchase salvation for us. Israel understood that the Messiah would be born to deliver them, but they didn't understand that He came to deliver all of humankind or that He would purchase our salvation with His death.

Salvation Army Bell Ringers

The folks who man (or woman) the familiar red kettles each holiday season, standing for hours in the chilly winter air to solicit donations for a very worthy cause by ringing bells for the Salvation Army (a Christian organization founded in 1865 by Methodist minister William Booth with headquarters in London, England). Many of the bell ringers are volunteers from local businesses, civic organizations, and schools; others are paid, some of them recruited from retirement homes, homeless shelters, and halfway houses. The bell ringers do not keep any portion of the money donated; and money raised funds shelters, after-school programs, toys for tots, emergency assistance, meal programs, and more. In recent years, some businesses that once welcomed the bell ringers and the big red kettles have restricted or banned them from the premises, a practice that has not gone over well with the public in general and that has even resulted in the boycott of some businesses by customers who want to see the familiar red kettle remain and who welcome the sound of the bells, which have helped ring in Christmas for so many years.

Salvation Army Santa

A bell ringer dressed as Santa Claus (*see* Salvation Army Bell Ringers).

Santa Claus

See Claus, Santa.

Santa's Sleigh

A sleigh is an open, usually horse-drawn vehicle. Santa's sleigh, however, is drawn by eight reindeer, except on foggy nights when Rudolph helps light the way with his glowing red nose (*see* Claus, Santa; *see also* Rudolph the Red-Nosed Reindeer).

Savior

Usually, whenever Christians talk about the "Savior," they are talking about Jesus Christ who gave Himself as a ransom for us so that we could be free from the consequences of sin and from eternal separation from God. Naturally, Christ is truly worthy of this title. However, the Bible also makes it clear that God the Father is equally responsible as the Savior of humankind. God made salvation possible by sending His Son into the world; and so through His Son Jesus, God is also the Savior of humankind. Likewise, the Holy Spirit's power is critical to our salvation, for He reveals the Father and the Son to humankind. So it is that we see every member of the Trinity at work in our salvation.

Scrooge

See Ebenezer Scrooge.

Scrooge, Ebenezer

See Ebenezer Scrooge.

Secret Santa

A "game" in which a group of people draw names and anonymously exchange gifts, often in the workplace or at church.

Seraphim

Angels who are members of the highest order of angels. In Isaiah's vision when he was called to the ministry, the celestial beings above God's throne (Isaiah 6:1–7). These are a different order of angels from the angels who heralded Christ's birth.

Sheep

In the Bible, humankind is often compared to this animal, which is easily led astray. Shepherds were watching over their flocks of sheep when they received the angels' announcement of Jesus' birth.

Shepherd

A person who tends, herds, and guards sheep. In the Bible, Christ is called "the Good Shepherd"; and as our Good Shepherd, He continues to search for each of His lost sheep—those of us who have gone astray (Matthew 18:12–14). Angels announced Jesus' birth to shepherds, who then went to Bethlehem to find the baby.

Shepherd's Crook

A long staff with the end curved to form a hook, used by shepherds to gently nudge stray sheep (Psalm 23:4).

Shofar

A ram's horn, used as a trumpet by the Hebrews in biblical times to announce certain religious occasions or to communicate signals in battle. In modern times, the shofar is used in synagogues chiefly during Rosh Hashanah and at the end of Yom Kippur.

Shopping

Visiting shops or stores and making Christmastime purchases (primarily for use as gifts). More and more, these purchases are being made online, due to the convenience of online shopping. Throughout the holiday season, we are constantly reminded by the media exactly how many shopping days are left until Christmas.

Trivia

In the film *Ernest Saves Christmas,* Ernest (Jim Varney) repeatedly mispronounces a reindeer's name. It was:

a. "Now Dasher, now Dancer, now Princess . . ."
b. ". . . now Prancer and Chicken . . ."
c. ". . . on Comet, on Stupid . . ."
d. ". . . on Donner and Blister . . ."

Silent Night A popular traditional Christmas carol composed in the early 1800s, with lyrics in German ("Stille Nacht") by Father Josef Mohr and music composed by Austrian Franz X. Gruber. There are a number of stories about the origin of the song. A popular origin story is that the church organ wasn't working, which is why the song was composed for guitar. No matter the origin, "Silent Night," as we have come to know the carol, is one of the prettiest and best loved of the Christmas carols.

Answer: D. Ernest needed to call each name correctly in order for the team to fly Santa's sleigh.

Silk

A lustrous fiber made from the cocoon of the silkworm. The word "silk" occurs a few times in the Bible; however, some scholars believe the Hebrew word for silk should be translated as "fine linen" or "costly fabric" (Proverbs 31:22; Ezekiel 16:10, 13). Silk is the fabric from which Frosty the Snowman's top hat was made (*see* Happy Birthday!!; *see also* Frosty the Snowman).

Silk Hat

A tall black hat, one of the most famous of which belonged to Frosty the Snowman (*see* Happy Birthday!!; *see also* Frosty the Snowman).

Simeon

There are four men named Simeon mentioned in the Bible. One of them was a faithful man who had been promised by God that he would not die until he saw the Messiah. Simeon recognized the infant Jesus when Mary and Joseph brought their baby to the temple to present Him to the Lord (Luke 2:25, 34).

Sin Transgression; disobedience to God or to His will for us; the thing that separates us from God. Because God loves us and wants us to be free from our sins, He sent His Son Jesus into the world. Through Jesus, atonement has been made for our sins so that we might be reconciled with God (Philippians 2:5–11).

Sing To produce a melodic sound, as to "sing" Christmas carols.

Sleigh Bells Small bells attached to the harness of animals drawing a sleigh or to the sleigh itself.

S'More A popular campfire treat, which consists of a toasted marshmallow with melted chocolate sandwiched between two graham crackers. The treat gets its name from the fact that once you have one, you will want "some more."

Snow

Precipitation in the form of ice crystals, which are formed from the freezing of water vapor in the air. This defines snow, but it doesn't begin to describe its beauty (*see* Snowflake).

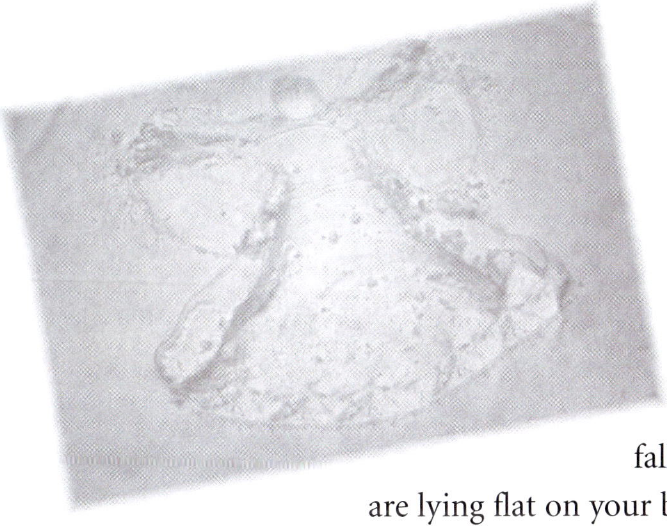

Snow Angel

To make a snow angel, first bundle up warmly; then, go outside and fall gently into the snow so that you are lying flat on your back. Next, brush your arms up and down between your head and waist in a sweeping motion; and move your legs as far apart as they will go and then back together. Repeat these motions until you have made impressions in the snow. Have someone help you up so that you can stand without stepping on your snow angel and so you don't leave a handprint in the middle of it. With care, you should end up with a beautiful angel in the snow.

Snowball Fights

For snowball fights, pack snow into balls and throw the balls at each other.

Snowflake

A particle of snow. We have all heard that no two snowflakes are alike. This was first discovered by snowflake photographer Wilson A. "Snowflake" Bentley (1865–1931) in the small town of Jericho, Vermont. Bentley was a pioneer in the area of photomicrography, particularly with snow crystals (snowflakes). His photographs were published in articles and magazines around the world; and in 1931, his book *Snow Crystals*, which featured more than 2,400 snowflake images, was published by McGraw-Hill. According to Bentley, he discovered under his microscope that snowflakes were miracles of beauty and every one a master of design, with no design ever repeated.

Snowman

A figure of a person made out of snow (*see* Frosty the Snowman).

Trivia

Which Old Testament prophet made this prediction: "'Behold, the virgin shall be with child, and bear a Son, and they shall call His name Immanuel,' which is translated, 'God with us' " (Matthew 1:23).

a. Isaiah
b. Daniel
c. Jeremiah
d. Samuel

Soldier

A person in the military service. At Christmas, one of the most familiar soldiers is the toy soldier or wooden soldier (*see* Babes in Toyland).

Solstice

Two times of the year when the sun is at its greatest distance from the equator. The Winter Solstice occurs around December 21 or 22 in the Northern Hemisphere. Many cultures celebrate a holiday around the time of the Winter Solstice, such as Kwanzaa, Hanukkah, and New Year (*see* Hanukkah; *see also* Kwanzaa).

Answer: A. Isaiah's complete prophecy is in the seventh chapter of the Book of Isaiah.

Some Assembly Required

To most parents, the words frequently found on the packaging of items that their little ones simply *must* have for Christmas are misleading (and dreaded). What are those words? "Some assembly required"!

Soot

A black powder produced during the incomplete combustion of objects like wood and coal. These fine particles adhere to the inside of a chimney; and according to Clement Moore's *'Twas the Night Before Christmas,* soot and ashes "tarnish" Santa's suit.

Spirit

In the Bible, "spirit" can refer to the human spirit—that part of us that is not flesh (Matthew 5:3; Romans 8:16; Hebrews 4:12). It can also refer to both good and evil spirits that are other than human, such as angels (Psalm 104:4) or evil spirits (Mark 9:25; Acts 19:12–17). Finally, "spirit" can refer to the Spirit of God, or the Holy Spirit (Acts 1:16; 2:16–21).

Sprinkles

Christmas sprinkles are fun toppings used in decorating holiday cupcakes, ice cream, and other goodies.

Squirrel

"Earl the Christmas Squirrel," a song by The Moffatts; also, *Earl and Pearl the Christmas Squirrels*, a book by Patrick John Rock.

Stable

A place (sometimes in a cave) where livestock are kept and fed. In biblical times, animals were often kept in stalls that were part of the house (in a two-story house, for example, the animals would have been kept on the ground floor, while the family lived in the second story). The Savior of humankind was born in a stable.

Stand

To be in an upright position. A Christmas tree stand holds the tree in an upright position. Open-air places for selling Christmas trees are also referred to as Christmas tree stands.

Star

A luminous heavenly body that appears at a fixed point each night. In the Bible, angels are also referred to as "morning stars" (Job 38:7). Wise men followed a star to find the One who had "been born King of the Jews" (Matthew 2:1, 2). That's why you'll often find stars used as tree toppers.

Star in the East

The Star of Bethlehem (*see* Star of Bethlehem).

Star of Bethlehem

The star mentioned in the Book of Matthew as God's sign of the birth of Jesus Christ. This is the star that was observed by the wise men from the East who came in search of the Messiah to worship Him (Matthew 2:2, 7, 9, 10). There are many scientific theories as to what the star may have been—everything from a supernova (exploding star) recorded by Chinese astronomers at about the time of the birth of Christ to a rare alignment of planets, which signaled an unusual event. Whatever the true explanation of this wondrous heavenly phenomenon, it led the wise men to Jesus (*see* Magi).

Stocking

Hung up at Christmas in hopes Santa will leave goodies in it. One of the origin stories claims that during the time of St. Nicholas in the fourth century, a widowed nobleman who could not afford a dowry for his daughter hung up one of the girl's stockings to dry. When St. Nicholas heard of the nobleman's plight, he threw a bag of gold through the man's window, which landed in the stocking. There are many other stories about the origin of the Christmas stocking tradition; none of them may actually be true. In North America, the first to show or mention Christmas stockings hung from a chimney were Thomas Nast in his illustrations in the late 1800s and writer George Webster in a story about Santa Claus.

Straw

The dried stalks of various grain. Straw made up the first bed of the infant Jesus, who was born in a stable.

String Cranberries

In days long ago, before trees were strung with electric lights, families would string cranberries together and decorate the tree with them. Popcorn would also be strung together to make decorations.

String Popcorn

See String Cranberries.

Stuffers

The goodies placed inside stockings.

Sugar Plum Fairy

A character from *The Nutcracker Ballet* (*see* Nutcracker).

Swaddling Bands

Long, narrow strips of cloth, much like bandages, that were used in wrapping newborns in Bible times.

Swaddling Cloths

See Swaddling Bands.

Sweater

A knitted garment, in pullover or cardigan style, with or without sleeves. At Christmas, sweaters are often decorated with symbols of the season, such as Christmas trees, snowmen, snowflakes, ornaments, reindeer, and Santa Claus. Many dads who are forced to wear brightly colored sweaters at Christmas wish their wives would not find the garments so appealing.

Swedish Foods

Swedish Christmas foods are a smorgasbord (a buffet meal of various foods) of delight, including sweets like saffron buns, soft ginger cakes, and ginger cookies in special Christmas shapes. In the middle of the Christmas "sweetie table" might be a pan for glogg (a hot wine punch) with special mugs and bowls of raisins and almonds to flavor the glogg.

Synagogue

A Jewish house of worship. The word literally translates “a leading or bringing together” and also refers to any assembly or gathering of the Jewish people. In Bible times, the synagogue was where the Jewish people would gather to read the Scriptures and to learn instruction on the Law of Moses.

Trivia

Myrrh is:

a. dried tree sap.
b. a Christian record label.
c. an expensive resin used in incense.
d. all of the above.

Answer: D. Myrrh was one of three gifts the wise men took to Jesus on their legendary sojourn.

T

Tax

A sum of money demanded by a government or ruling body. In the Bible, taxes may have originated with the custom of giving gifts in exchange for being protected from harm (Genesis 32:13–21; 33:10; 43:11). During Jesus' time, it is believed the Jewish people were paying approximately 30 to 40 percent of their income for taxes and religious dues.

Thanksgiving, The Friday After

See Black Friday.

Three French Hens

In the religious interpretation of the song "Twelve Days of Christmas," the three French hens are said to represent Faith, Hope, and Love (*see* Twelve Days of Christmas).

Three Kings Day

Celebrated on January 6 (*see* Epiphany).

Tidings

News or information. In the Bible, “good tidings of great joy” was the news of the birth of Jesus Christ (Luke 2:9, 10).

Tinsel

Thin strips of a shining substance, frequently silver or gold in color, used to decorate a Christmas tree.

Tiny Tim

An endearing character from Charles Dickens’s *A Christmas Carol*, this tiny, sickly boy helps to change the heart of Ebenezer Scrooge (*see* A Christmas Carol).

Top 10 Gifts

The list of Top 10 Gifts changes from year to year. What is a “Top 10” gift this year for Christmas may not even be on the list next year. This is why the best, most enduring gifts you can give for the holiday season are those that are never out of season—gifts such as love, friendship, and kindness to others.

Toys

A child's playthings. Some toys (e.g., dolls, whistles, balls) have stood the test of time and are always popular. Children look forward to receiving toys from Santa on Christmas morning.

Traditions

Customs, beliefs, celebrations, and practices that are handed down from one generation to the next. Many traditions connected with Christmas add meaning and enjoyment to the season. Christmas Eve Communion and Christmas Nativity pageants are two such traditions.

Treats

Special rewards or pleasures; often referring to sweet goodies such as cake, candies, cookies, or ice cream.

Tree

A branched plant with a woody main stem or trunk, which may grow to considerable height (*see* Christmas Tree).

Trivia

You're in Greenland eating a traditional Christmas food called kiviak. What is it?

a. Eel, pureed in seal oil.
b. A dessert of shortbread layers soaked in coffee.
c. Mostly decomposed, raw poultry wrapped in a seal skin.
d. A whole sheep's head, eyes included.

Tree of Knowledge

The tree in the Garden of Eden that bore the fruit forbidden to Adam and Eve, but of which they ate (Genesis 2:17; 3:6–24). *See* Christmas Tree.

Tree of Life

In the Garden of Eden, the tree whose fruit gave everlasting life to those who ate it. This tree was not forbidden to Adam and Eve until after they ate from the Tree of Knowledge and were banished from the garden (Genesis 2:9; 3:22). *See* Christmas Tree.

Answer: C. Kiviak is made by wrapping the raw flesh of an auk in seal skin, then burying it under a stone for several months.

Trim the Tree

Decorate the Christmas tree (*see* Christmas Tree).

Truth

The actual state or meaning of a matter. In both the Old and New Testaments, truth is one of the moral characteristics of God. Jesus is "the way, the truth, and the life. No one comes to the Father except through [Him]" (John 14:6).

Turkey

A large bird that traditionally finds its way onto the holiday menu at both Thanksgiving and Christmas in the United States.

Turtledoves

Small European doves, which have soft, purring voices (*see* Twelve Days of Christmas).

Twelfth Night

Among some Christians a holiday that marks the coming of Epiphany. In some cultures, the celebration of Epiphany is marked by the exchange of gifts; and Twelfth Night takes on the same significance as Christmas Eve (*see* Epiphany).

Twelve Days of Christmas

The 12 Days of Christmas are not the 12 days before Christmas, as many people think. For most of the Western Church, the 12 days are from December 25 to January 6 (Epiphany, or the day observed as the day the Three Wise Men brought gifts to thc infant Jesus). However, some cultures observe December 26 as the first day of Christmas, and January 6 is held as a special day (in Hispanic culture, it's known as the Day of the Kings, and gifts are often exchanged on this day).

"The Twelve Days of Christmas" is also the title of a popular Christmas carol which has a history steeped in legend and myth. While the song has long been considered a traditional English carol, there is some evidence that it may be French in origin. There are also some who believe that the song contains hidden references to the Christian faith and may have been used as far back as the 16th century as a mnemonic device to preserve and teach the principles of the Catholic faith, during a time when religious wars raged and it was unsafe to profess openly certain religious beliefs. The proponents of this theory believe that what they perceive as symbolism in the song can be interpreted as follows:

A partridge in a pear tree (Jesus Christ, symbolically the mother partridge who clucks over and protects her chicks, Luke 13:34)

Two turtledoves (The Old and New Testaments)

Three French hens (Faith, Hope, and Love, 1 Corinthians 13:13)

Four calling birds (The Four Gospels, Matthew, Mark, Luke, and John)

Five gold(en) rings (The first five books of the Old Testament, known as the Torah or Pentateuch)

Six geese a' laying (The six days of creation)

Seven swans a' swimming (The seven gifts of the Spirit, Romans 12:6–8)

Eight maids a' milking (The Beatitudes, Matthew 5:3–10)

Nine ladies dancing (Nine fruits of the Spirit, Galatians 5:22, 23)

Ten lords a'leaping (The 10 commandments, Exodus 20:1–17)

Eleven pipers piping (The 11 faithful apostles; Judas, the apostle who betrayed Jesus, is not included)

Twelve drummers drumming (The 12 points in the Apostles' Creed)

Some believe that the *true love* mentioned in the song represents God the Father. While there is nothing substantive to support the history attributed to the religious symbolism of this Christmas carol, neither has it been disproved.

Trivia

You decide to spend the holidays on Christmas Island. Where are you?

a. The Caribbean
b. In Australian territory
c. The French Riviera
d. The North Pole

Answer: B. Christmas Island is a tropical Australian territory about 300 miles south of Jakarta, Indonesia.

Ugg Boots

A generic term for a type of sheepskin boot, which originated in Australia and is worn in cold weather. While Santa wears his traditional black boots, it's rumored that Mrs. Claus prefers to brave North Pole winters in her ugg boots.

Umble Pie

Pie was a popular medieval dish eaten at Christmas in England. Umble pie dates back to the time of William the Conqueror and refers to pie made from the umbles, that is, from the heart, gizzard, and liver of a deer. This dish was served to the servants and huntsmen, while the lord of the manor dined on venison; therefore, one who ate umble pie was in an inferior or subservient position.

Trivia

In *The Best Christmas Pageant Ever,* the Herdmans hated the idea of giving baby Jesus gold, frankincense, and myrrh. What did they bring Him instead?

a. A ham
b. Gym socks
c. Their cat
d. Cigars

Answer: A. The Herdmans decided Jesus was better off with the Christmas ham they'd gotten from charity.

V

Vestments Garments worn by clergy in certain Christian traditions during services. The colors of these garments often correspond to the season of the church year being celebrated. The color for Advent, for example, would be different from the color for Lent.

Virgin A person who has never had sexual intercourse. In the Old Testament, it was prophesied that the mother of the Messiah would be a virgin (Isaiah 7:14). When Mary conceived Jesus, the prophecy was fulfilled (Matthew 1:23).

Virgin Birth The doctrine that by the miraculous agency of God, Jesus Christ was born of Mary, a virgin (Luke 1:26–38). This divine birth had been foretold by the prophet Isaiah (Isaiah 7:14) and could only have been accomplished by God Himself. It was a miracle that distinguished Jesus' birth from all others, before or since.

Virginia

In 1897, an eight-year-old girl named Virginia O'Hanlon wrote to the *New York Sun*, a prominent New York City newspaper, and asked if there was a Santa Claus (some of her friends had caused her to doubt his existence). One of the newspaper's editors, Francis P. Church, responded to Virginia's letter with an editorial that became one of the most famous editorials ever written. His phrase "Yes, Virginia, there is a Santa Claus" became an oft-repeated one; and throughout her life, Virginia O'Hanlon continued to receive correspondence about her famous letter.

Vision

A mystical, supernatural experience similar to dreams in which insight or knowledge is given by revelation. In the Bible, people who experienced visions had a special awareness of God. There were many who experienced visions, including Daniel, whose vision foretold the coming of the Messiah (Daniel 9:24–27).

Wassail

A punch made of heated wine or sweetened ale and spices and often served at Christmastime.

We Three Kings of Orient Are

A Christmas carol written in 1857 by Rev. John Henry Hopkins, Jr., as part of a Christmas pageant. The song is about the wise men who traveled from afar to find the infant Jesus (*see* Magi).

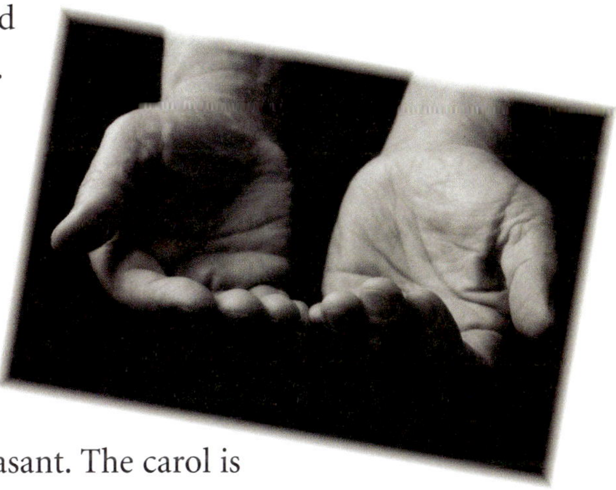

Wenceslas

"Good King Wenceslas" is a popular Christmas carol about a king who goes out on St. Stephen's Day (December 26, also known as Boxing Day in the UK) and gives alms to a poor peasant. The carol is from the 1800s and is based on the historical figure Saint Wenceslas I, Duke of Bohemia (907–935). *See* Boxing Day.

White Christmas

See Crosby, Bing.

White Elephant

Something that is unwanted by the owner but difficult to dispose of. Unfortunately, some of the gifts we are given at Christmas fall into this category. We can't dispose of them or even regift them because they were given to us by people who care about us and who meant well in giving us these gifts.

Wings

In the Bible, God is described as protecting His people under His wings (Ruth 2:12; Psalm 17:8). And God's angels are often portrayed as having mighty wings (Ezekiel 10:4, 5).

Winter Wonderland

A popular Christmas song written in 1934 by Felix Bernard and Roger Smith. The song has been recorded many times by various artists; and while it does not mention Christmas specifically, it has become a standard enjoyed by all during the holiday season.

Wise Men

See Magi.

Word

In the Bible, the Word is Jesus Christ. "And the Word became flesh and dwelt among us" (John 1:14).

Word of God

The means by which God makes Himself known and declares His will.

Worship

Reverent homage paid to God or to an object of worship. For Christians, one of the ways we worship is through praise (*see* Praise). When the wise men finally found the young Christ Child, they worshiped Him by presenting Him with costly gifts (Matthew 2:11).

Wrapping Paper

Paper used for wrapping packages and gifts. At Christmas, special wrapping papers are printed with winter and holiday motifs.

Wreath

A garland of greenery used as a decoration. Particularly popular during the Christmas season, wreaths are often displayed on windows and doors.

Writer's Cramp

Something you will most probably get after addressing all those Christmas cards.

Trivia

Which is the top-grossing, Christmas-themed movie in the United States?

a. *How the Grinch Stole Christmas* (2000 version)
b. *Home Alone*
c. *The Polar Express*
d. *The Santa Clause 2*

Answer: B. The original *Home Alone* raked in more than $285 million at the box office and earned two Oscar nods.

X

Xmas

Some are offended by the abbreviation "Xmas" and feel that it is taking the Christ out of Christmas. However, for centuries (about 1,000 years), people have abbreviated the Greek word for "Christ" as either Xt or XP (X and P are derived from the uppercase versions of two Greek letters). During the 1500s, "Xian" was used as an abbreviation for Christian, and "Xianity" as an abbreviation for Christianity. The letter "X" has been with us a long time as a representation for Christ. However you prefer to write it, "Christmas" or "Xmas," the holiday still belongs to Christ.

Xylophone

A musical instrument with a series of wooden bars of varying lengths that produce the musical scale; music is made by striking the bars with two small wooden hammers.

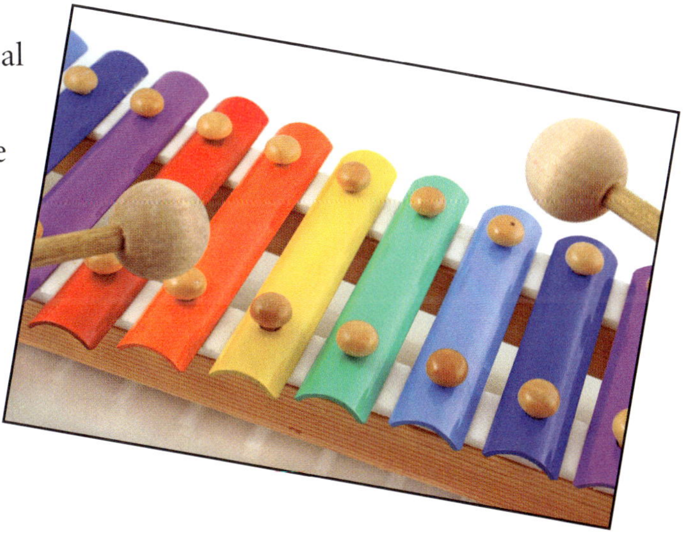

Trivia

You're walking in a store and hear the familiar Salvation Army bell ringers. When you drop your dollar, you notice the receptacle is always:

a. A red kettle.
b. A red can.
c. A green kettle.
d. A red ceramic pail.

Answer: A. The Salvation Army has used red kettles to collect for the poor since 1891.

Yeshua The Hebrew name *Yeshua* is *Iēsous* in Greek, from which we get the name "Jesus." Its root means "to deliver" or "to save."

YHWH Known as the Hebrew Tetragrammaton, the personal name of the God of Israel (*see* Lord).

You'll Shoot Your Eye Out The warning given to Ralphie Parker by virtually every adult in *A Christmas Story* (*see* A Christmas Story).

Yule The Christmas season; the feast of the birth of Jesus Christ.

Yule Log

A large wooden log that was traditionally cut and carried to the house on Christmas Eve, where the master of the house would place it on the hearth. The young girls of the house (or sometimes the mother) would light the log with splinters that had been saved from the preceding year's log. The custom of the Yule log dates back to the 12th century, and it was known in most European countries. Today, the Yule log has become a traditional and delicious cake pastry, smothered in chocolate or coffee flavored icing and decorated with sugared roses and holly leaves.

Yuletide

See Yule.

Z

Zacharias

There are two men mentioned in the Bible by the name of Zacharias. One was the prophet who was murdered because he rebuked God's people for breaking the Lord's commandments (Luke 11:51). The other was the father of John the Baptist (Luke 1:13; 3:2).

Zamboni

A machine that resurfaces the ice on a skating rink. During Christmases past, no such machine existed, and the idyllic scenes of ice skaters and the skating ponds that we see on Currier & Ives Christmas cards were the result of Old Man Winter and Mother Nature, not a machine.

Zip Codes with Christmas Name

Some but by no means all: North Pole, Alaska 99705; Santa Claus, Indiana 47579; Christmas, Florida 32709; Santa Claus, Georgia 30436; Christmas, Michigan 49862; Christmas Valley, Oregon 97641.

Zoo

A park area in which animals are kept in cages. Also, the chaos left after the kiddies have opened their presents on Christmas morning.

Zwarte Piet

Translates "Black Pete" and in Dutch folklore is a helper to St. Nicholas; his counterpart in western culture would be the elves who assist Santa Claus.

More Trivia

(answers on page 202)

1. Handel wrote *Messiah* to get people thinking about Jesus during:

    a. Hard times.
    b. Easter and Christmas.
    c. Lent.
    d. Holy days and church feasts.

2. In the Gospels, when Mary visited her cousin Elizabeth, Mary was pregnant with Jesus, and Elizabeth with:

    a. Judas Iscariot.
    b. James the Apostle.
    c. Harold Angel.
    d. John the Baptist.

3. Match these Christmas songs and origins:

a.	"The Virgin Mary Had a Baby Boy"	Germany
b.	"Carol of the Bells"	Trinidad
c.	"O Christmas Tree"	England
d.	"I Saw Three Ships"	Ukraine

4. Which company puts an index with each box of chocolates that identifies their fillings?

   a. Hershey's
   b. Russell Stover
   c. Whitman's
   d. Palmer's

5. Match the popular toy with the year it was first sold:

a.	View-Master 3-D Viewer	1933
b.	Silly Putty	1938
c.	G.I. Joe	1950
d.	Monopoly	1964

6. What are "swaddling cloths" ?

   a. Middle-eastern onesies, probably a gift from the shepherds.
   b. Narrow strips of cloth used to wrap a baby tightly, like a burrito.
   c. A baby's first tunic, woven as one piece.
   d. Probably Mary's headdress since there was no bedding.

7. In *National Lampoon's Christmas Vacation,* Clark (Chevy Chase) asks Aunt Bethany to say grace over the meal. She:

   a. recites the Pledge of Allegiance.
   b. sings the national anthem.
   c. is dead, but the family thinks she's napping.
   d. performs "Rapper's Delight."

8. Until about 1840, many Americans rejected this tradition, believing it a pagan symbol:

   a. Christmas wreaths
   b. Christmas presents
   c. Christmas trees
   d. Father Christmas

1. Answer: B. Handel's renowned, Scripture-heavy oratorio was later divided into sections that performers usually tackled at either Easter or Christmas.
2. Answer: D. Read about how the unborn John the Baptist reacted to the unborn Christ in the first chapter of the Gospel of Luke.
3. Answers: A = Trinidad; B = Ukraine; C = Germany; D = England
4. Answer: C. The Whitman's Sampler box containing the informative chart debuted in 1912.
5. Answers: A = 1938; B = 1950; C = 1964 ; D = 1933
6. Answer: B. Swaddling is the ancient practice of restricting infant movement.
7. Answer: A. Aunt Bethany's prayer randomly takes a patriotic spin.
8. Answer: C. The Christmas tree finally gained popularity in the U.S. around 1890.